BLACK+DECKER™

CARPENTRY MADE SIMPLE

23 Stylish Projects • Learn as You Build

COOL
SPRINGS
PRESS

Inspiring | Educating | Creating | Entertaining

Brimming with creative inspiration, how-to projects, and useful information to enrich your everyday life, Quarto Knows is a favourite destination for those pursuing their interests and passions. Visit our site and dig deeper with our books into your area of interest: Quarto Creates, Quarto Cooks, Quarto Homes, Quarto Lives, Quarto Drives, Quarto Explores, Quarto Gifts, or Quarto Kids.

© 2018 Quarto Publishing Group USA Inc.

First published in 2018 by Cool Springs Press, an imprint of The Quarto Group, 401 Second Avenue North, Suite 310, Minneapolis, MN 55401 USA. T: (612) 344-8100 F: (612) 344-8692 www.QuartoKnows.com

All rights reserved. No part of this book may be reproduced in any form without written permission of the copyright owners. All images in this book have been reproduced with the knowledge and prior consent of the artists concerned, and no responsibility is accepted by producer, publisher, or printer for any infringement of copyright or otherwise, arising from the contents of this publication. Every effort has been made to ensure that credits accurately comply with information supplied. We apologize for any inaccuracies that may have occurred and will resolve inaccurate or missing information in a subsequent reprinting of the book.

Cool Springs Press titles are also available at discount for retail, wholesale, promotional, and bulk purchase. For details, contact the Special Sales Manager by email at specialsales@quarto.com or by mail at The Quarto Group, Attn: Special Sales Manager, 401 Second Avenue North, Suite 310, Minneapolis, MN 55401 USA.

10 9 8 7 6 5 4 3 2 1

ISBN: 978-0-7603-5779-8

Library of Congress Cataloging-in-Publication Data
Names: Cool Springs Press, issuing body. | Black & Decker Corporation (Towson, Md.), contributor.
Title: Black & Decker custom grills & smokers : build your own backyard cooking & tailgating equipment / by editors of Cool Springs Press.
Other titles: Black and Decker custom grills and smokers
Description: Minneapolis, Minnesota : Cool Springs Press, [2017] | Includes bibliographical references and index.
Identifiers: LCCN 2017030791 | ISBN 9780760353547 (pb)
Subjects: LCSH: Outdoor cooking. | Barbecues (Fireplaces) | Gas grills.
Classification: LCC TX840.B3 B5566 2017 | DDC 641.5/78--dc23
LC record available at https://lccn.loc.gov/2017030791

Acquiring Editor: Mark Johanson
Project Manager: Jordan Wiklund
Art Director: James Kegley
Photography: Rich Fleischman
Layout: Kim Winscher

Printed in China

MIX
Paper from responsible sources
FSC® C016973

BLACK+DECKER and the BLACK+DECKER logo are trademarks of The Black & Decker Corporation and are used under license. All rights reserved.

NOTICE TO READERS

For safety, use caution, care, and good judgment when following the procedures described in this book. The publisher and BLACK+DECKER cannot assume responsibility for any damage to property or injury to persons as a result of misuse of the information provided.

The techniques shown in this book are general techniques for various applications. In some instances, additional techniques not shown in this book may be required. Always follow manufacturers' instructions included with products, since deviating from the directions may void warranties. The projects in this book vary widely as to skill levels required: some may not be appropriate for all do-it-yourselfers, and some may require professional help.

Consult your local building department for information on building permits, codes, and other laws as they apply to your project.

CONTENTS

Introduction

Making useful, attractive furniture from wood is a skill for the novice as well as the experienced craftsman who has been plying his trade for decades. When we learn to talk, we start with sounds and progress to words and sentences. Building with wood is no different. We start with inspiration, learn a couple basic skills, and grow from there.

Woodworkers have been devising ways to make things easier, safer, and more accurate for centuries. With this book, my hope is that you'll find inspiration not only in simple, elegant furniture, but also in the tips, jigs, and essential skills that I have found useful over the last thirty years. A handful of good tips and methods of work can open up worlds of possibilities.

You may not own all the tools in this book, but I've tried to keep to a pretty basic tool kit. Where practical, I'll give you an alternative method using a more common tool than the one shown. The acquisition of more and better tools as you need or can afford them, like the skill in using them, takes time. Buy the best quality tools that you can afford. That said, the best chisel isn't necessarily the $50 hand-forged variety. It may be a beautiful, quality tool, but you can do the same work with a $5 chisel that you keep razor sharp.

The 23 projects shown with complete plans in this book are arranged (more or less) in ascending complexity, starting with the basic two-board X-Chair. With each project I have highlighted one or two skills, materials, or tools that are key components of the process. The intent here is to create kind of a protracted "course" in home carpentry where you can add a new arrow to your carpentry quiver and build your skills with each project. Of course, it is not likely that anyone would make all 23 of the projects, but I do encourage you to read through the book from start to finish and follow along as the information accumulates.

My hope is also that as you learn the fundamental techniques, you'll feel free to revise designs and come up with methods of work that suit you. You'll make mistakes, you'll find ways to fix them, and you'll end up having made something useful and beautiful.

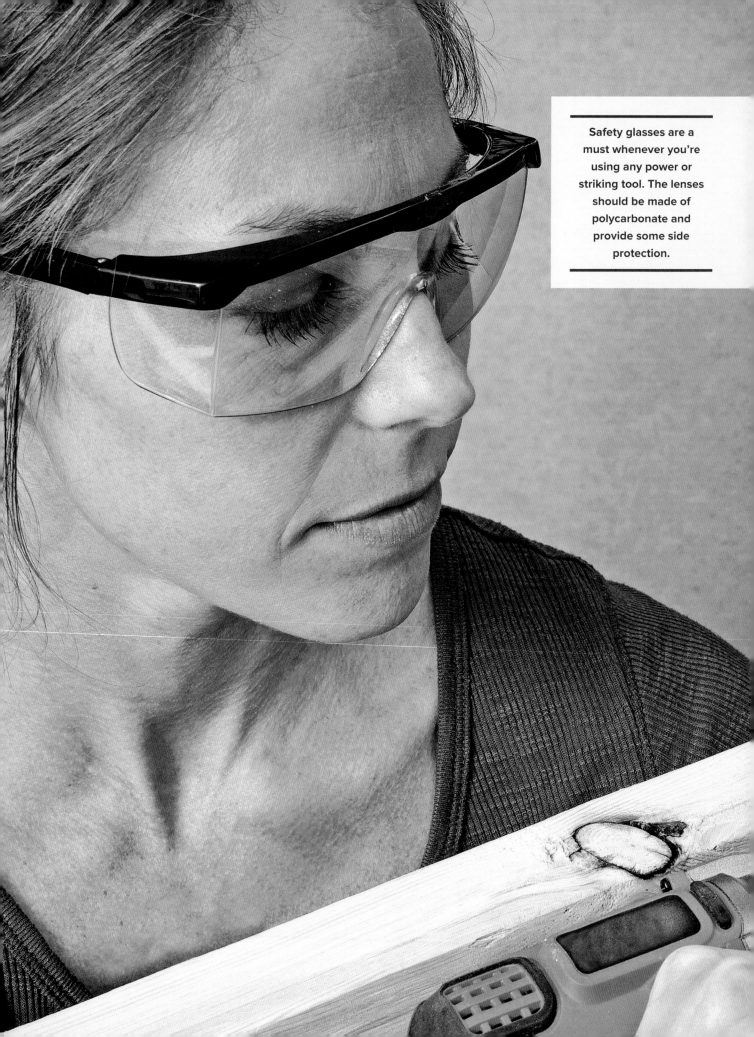

Safety glasses are a must whenever you're using any power or striking tool. The lenses should be made of polycarbonate and provide some side protection.

Personal Safety

The threat of personal injury in a workshop is not something anyone wants to think about, but taking care with your personal safety is essential to making your shop experience a pleasant and productive one. It really doesn't take that much effort to look after your own well-being, and unsafe practices and a hazardous shop environment can be distracting and have a negative effect on your work. Establishing good work habits and a patient attitude will ensure that you're actively staying safe, while the basic safety gear that protects your eyes, ears, lungs, and hands provides essential passive backup.

EYE PROTECTION

It's a good idea to get into the habit of wearing safety glasses whenever you use power tools or do any finishing. Most tool manufacturers, for example, insist on it as a condition for using their tools—hand tools as well as power tools.

Safety glasses and goggles offer more protection than standard eyeglasses. Their lenses are made of polycarbonate, which is more impact resistant than acrylic, the standard material for corrective lenses. Look for the high-impact Z87+ rating on the frames. Even if your regular glasses have polycarbonate lenses, safety glasses typically have larger lenses that provide more coverage and often wrap around or have side shields for greater protection. Safety glasses with tinted lenses are available for outdoor use, and prescription safety glasses can be purchased at many optical shops.

Goggles add another layer of protection with a seal between the glasses frame and your face—a very real advantage when working with

Various types of eye and face protection are made for different types of work. For instance, goggles are needed when working with some liquids and when there's a lot of debris in the air.

chemicals or in very dusty environments. And if you're grinding metal or doing wood turning, you should wear a full-face shield.

HEARING PROTECTION

Power tools can literally be deafening—more than a few lifetime woodworkers have seen their hearing ruined after years of working with high-pitch tools while not protecting their hearing. Although some tools are louder than others, even short-term exposure to high-pitched motor noise can cause hearing loss. It's generally accepted that a sustained noise level above 85 decibels over time can cause permanent damage, and tools such as routers, shop vacuums, and circular saws can easily exceed that level.

There are basically two types of hearing protectors: earplugs, which fit into the ear canal, and earmuffs, which cover the entire ear. When used properly, they block about the

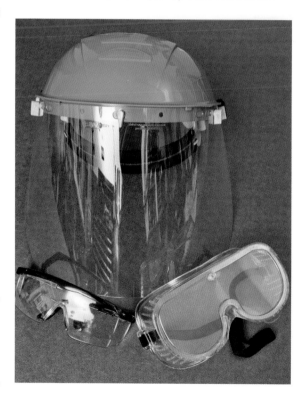

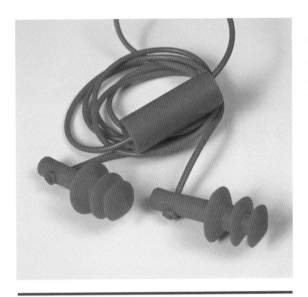

Earplugs are best for blocking low frequencies, but you can wear them with muffs to cover all the bases.

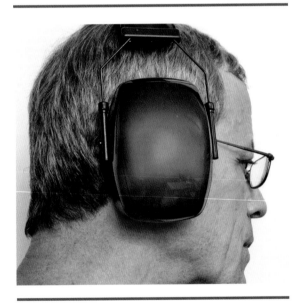

Earmuffs are good at blocking high-frequency sound, so they're your best choice when operating tools such as routers, sanders, and vacuums.

same amount of noise—from about 15 to 30 decibels—but muffs block high frequencies better, while plugs are more effective at blocking low frequencies.

Earplugs are more convenient because they're small, they're often very inexpensive, and it's easy to get them to seal tightly in the ear canal. The least expensive plugs are the disposable foam variety. The more durable and often more effective silicone earplugs are also available with a leash that keeps them conveniently draped around your neck.

Good earmuffs should have soft ear cushions that conform around your head snugly but comfortably to block sound. The headband should be padded, adjustable, and articulated to provide a good, comfortable fit. Some muffs even offer built-in sound canceling, a radio, and the option to plug in a personal listening device. In extremely noisy situations, such as around construction sites, both plugs and muffs can be used at the same time for maximum effect.

BREATHING PROTECTION

Protecting your lungs from dust and fumes is the job of particulate (dust) masks and respirators (gas masks), respectively. And just like hearing protectors, they need to fit snugly around both your mouth and your nose to function properly. A loose-fitting dust mask will let dust enter around the sides, and an ill-fitting or poorly adjusted respirator won't keep fumes out of your lungs.

Masks are often rated by the National Institute for Occupational Safety and Health (NIOSH) and the Mine Safety Health Administration (MSHA) for their function and effectiveness at filtering out fine particles. Good disposable dust masks have an adjustable nose clip and some also have a valve that improves comfort by expelling exhaled air. You'll want to be sure the mask doesn't interfere with your eye or ear protection and that it's comfortable to wear for extended periods.

If the dust collection on the tool you're using is highly effective, you may not need to wear a mask. But it's almost impossible to collect all airborne dust when using lathes, jigsaws, miter saws, most sanders, and a few other tools.

A particulate dust mask should be worn in dusty environments, but it's not effective for filtering vapors from finishes.

Face shields provide the protection you need when doing lathe work and some metalworking.

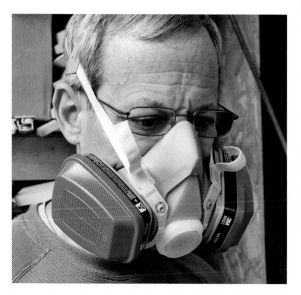

To filter volatile organic compounds (VOCs), often contained in finishing products, you should wear a respirator.

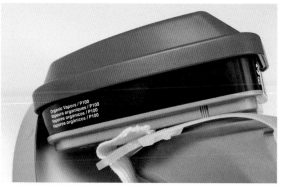

The label on a respirator cartridge will provide information about its use. If you can smell fumes through the mask, it's time to replace the cartridges.

Finding the right respirator for your needs requires a little more attention. Most masks use two cartridges that are made to remove a variety of hazardous materials, such as VOCs, toxic dust, and acid gas. It's important to use the correct cartridges for your job and dispose of them when they're spent. If you can smell fumes through the mask, the cartridges need to be replaced. Respirators usually have a pre-filter to keep larger particles out of the cartridges, so you can also use it as a dust mask in a pinch. Disposable respirators are an option if you do a limited amount of finishing work. They'll last for several finishing sessions and cost less than masks that use replaceable cartridges.

Some respirators have an integrated full-face shield, which is a nice feature to have to keep mist and particles out of your eyes if you're spray painting. Of course, a mask's fit is key to its effectiveness and comfort, so a mask with a silicone face piece is usually your best bet. Silicone is more conforming and comfortable than the plastics used on cheaper masks.

HAND PROTECTION

There are jobs when it makes sense to wear gloves, and there are times when you should never wear them. If you're working in close proximity to a moving blade or workpiece, you should take off the gloves for better dexterity. A blade can catch a glove and pull your hand into it, and that can cause a far more serious injury than might happen without gloves.

Specifically, avoid wearing gloves when using a tablesaw, a bandsaw, a lathe, a belt sander, a router, and similar tools. For that matter, avoid wearing loose-fitting clothing of any kind when working with power tools. There's too much chance they can get caught and pull you into the cutter.

But gloves should be worn to give your hands a needed break and save them from wear and tear when handling lumber, sanding, applying finishes, and doing cleanup chores.

Leather gloves afford the most protection when working with lumber, and rough stock in particular. They'll guard against splinters and blisters, but they can get warm if worn for long periods.

Cloth and leather gloves provide more ventilation and can work for similar jobs. There are numerous brands of work gloves with hybrid synthetic and leather construction that have a trim fit and job-specific features—such as materials with extra traction for an enhanced grip, abrasion protection for extended life, and padding for vibration reduction.

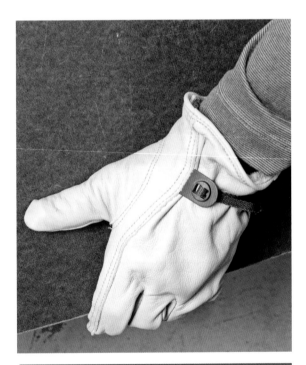

Leather work gloves provide excellent protection for carrying lumber.

Knit rubber-coated gloves are relatively cool to wear and they're useful for many shop applications, including finishing.

Disposable nitrile exam gloves are handy to have around for applying water-based finishes and cleaning up liquid spills. But if you're using solvent-base finishes, you should use thicker nitrile gloves.

Some other useful gloves to have around the shop include knit cotton bricklayer's gloves with rubberized grips, Kevlar or stainless-steel chain-mail gloves that provide cut protection for woodcarving and close detail work with chisels, and fingerless gloves that protect your palm without compromising dexterity.

FIRE PREVENTION

Beyond personal protection gear there are a number of items that should be in your shop to ensure safety. The most important of these is a multipurpose ABC fire extinguisher. This type of extinguisher uses dry chemicals that can fight fires caused by common combustibles (wood, paper, cloth), chemicals (liquid finishing products), and electrical equipment (motors, wiring). To be on the safe side, you should have more than one, storing them in easily accessible locations and not hidden behind other equipment.

A smoke detector or combination smoke detector/carbon monoxide (CO) alarm goes hand-in-glove with the fire extinguisher. A combination alarm makes the most sense if you have a furnace or heater in your shop, but this type of alarm also provides a more reliable and responsive system for detecting fires. Most alarms are battery operated, but some are hardwired with a battery backup, although the battery-only units offer the best installation flexibility.

An ABC fire extinguisher will extinguish most types of fires. Be sure to mount it in an obvious, easy-to-reach location.

Shops are susceptible to fires, so a smoke/CO detector is essential and may be required by code in some communities. Models shown here include: (A) hard-wired CO detector; (B) ionizing smoke detector; (C) photoelectric smoke detector; (D) heat-activated fire detector.

The average life of an alarm is about seven years, and it must be replaced once it quits functioning. All alarms have an end-of-life and a low-battery warning, so you'll never be left unprotected. In some communities, smoke/CO detectors may be required in home shops by code, so check with your local code authority.

FIRST AID

It's inevitable that you'll suffer an occasional self-inflicted cut or splinter, so it pays to be prepared with a first-aid kit. Most shop injuries are minor and can be dealt with on the spot. There's no need to go overboard—you won't be performing surgery—so a basic kit should be all you need. At minimum, the kit should include bandages in several shapes and sizes, gauze pads, sterile eye pads, alcohol pads, antiseptic or antibiotic ointment, bandage tape, small scissors, tweezers, exam gloves, cotton swabs, and over-the-counter pain medication.

In the case of a more serious injury, such as one that bleeds profusely or is quite deep, don't try to tend to it yourself—it's not a DIY project and requires the attention of a healthcare professional. What's really important is to

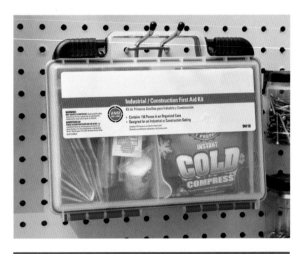

Should an accident happen, it pays to be prepared with a first-aid kit that's equipped specifically for shop mishaps.

remember that accidents most often happen for reasons such as losing focus, rushing through work, and becoming distracted or impatient. If an accident does happen—even a small one—take a break, gather your composure, and eat a light snack. For that matter, make a habit of taking regular breaks to help prevent mishaps.

But sometimes things just get out of control and you need to summon help, so keep your cell phone close at hand with the numbers of physicians, hospitals, urgent-care facilities, and 911 on speed dial.

TOOL SAFETY FEATURES

Removing accident-causing variables from your work routine is another way keep you out of trouble. There are some basic shop safety devices that should be standard equipment in your shop, on your workbench, and at stationary machines.

Push sticks or push pads are essential for guiding stock close to blades and bits on tablesaws, bandsaws, jointers, and router tables. They allow you to maintain steady pressure and direction on the workpiece while keeping your hands a safe distance from the cutter. Commercially made push sticks are available in a variety of shapes, or you can make your own out of wood or plastic.

Attempting to hold or stabilize a workpiece with one hand while using a tool with the other is almost always an accident waiting to happen.

Bench dogs and stops are most often associated with high-end cabinetmaker's benches to stabilize larger workpieces, but they're easy to make and install on any basic bench with a solid top. Simply use ¾-inch dowels and bore holes for them in the bench top. Then glue and screw small blocks on top of the dowels to prevent them from falling through the holes. When used together with clamps on the edge of the bench, they'll secure the work and keep it from moving when sawing, routing, and sanding.

Along the same lines as bench dogs, bench vises are generally used to secure smaller pieces and are a must-have fixture for all shops. Some are mounted to the edge of the bench top and others can be bolted to the top. They have an almost unlimited range of uses, including holding work for planing, drilling, routing, and gluing. Some edge-mounted vises with built-in dogs can also be used in conjunction with bench dogs to clamp or hold long workpieces. For this to work, the top of the vise must be level with the bench top and in line with the bench dog stations on the top.

Other devices that are usually included with stationary tools, such as guards and miter gauge, should be used when appropriate. When setting blade exposure on any tool, it should be the minimum amount possible while still being able to make a successful cut.

You may occasionally have visitors in your shop, and they need to be as aware of your shop safety rules as you are. Make it clear to anyone entering your shop while you're using a power tool that they should not interrupt in any way that might startle you. And if they enter unannounced,

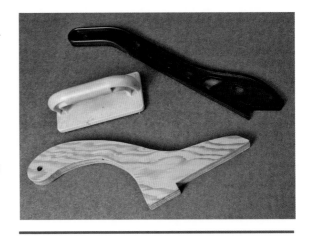

Push sticks and push block/pads should be standard equipment around all shop machinery. They'll keep your hands a safe distance from spinning blades and cutters.

they should stand clear until you've completed the work and not try to assist you unless you request it.

Bench dogs aren't just a luxury for fancy workbenches; they can stabilize workpieces and keep them from unexpectedly sliding out from under a tool.

A bench vise holds workpieces so you don't have to. And it makes sense to have more than one for different types and sizes of work.

X-Chair

This chair is one of my favorite designs—no pretense, no fasteners, the picture of portable simplicity.

I've always been a bit intimidated by designing and building chairs. There are so many elements to take into account. Proportions and angles have to be just right, as an uncomfortable chair is a

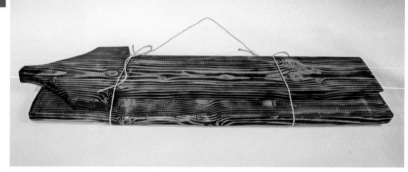

Because this chair consists of just two boards that are fitted together via a slot, the chair is fully portable. But if you'll be moving it around, rig up a rope handle to make it easier to transport.

failure by any measure. This chair, boiled down to the bare essentials of seating, removes any whiff of intimidation. And if it doesn't turn out quite right the first time, the investment is paltry. In spite of its simplicity, once you've fitted it to suit your stature, it's surprisingly comfortable. And perhaps best of all it breaks down easily into two boards that can be toted to any picnic or perhaps even your favorite Renfest. (It is a very old design.)

X-CHAIR SHOPPING LIST

1: 2 × 12 × 96
Construction-grade lumber*

▶ **Finishing materials**
(Spar varnish—a nautical finish—was used here.)

∗ WOOD SELECTION: Choose Douglas fir if your local lumber supplier carries it. Or you may use any of the more common "SPF" lumbers (spruce-pine-fir), which are called "whitewood" by some sellers. None of these species is exterior-rated, but they are strong. If your chair will be exposed to the elements, apply a UV-and-moisture-resistant finish. You may also use cedar or cypress to make the chair, both of which are naturally moisture-resistant and may be left unfinished. (They will turn gray over time.) Both species are softer and more splinter-prone than the "SPF" varieties, however, so your chair may not last as long.

Or, you can choose pressure-treated lumber. Some DIYers are reluctant to use chemical-treated lumber, but today's generation of preservatives are far less toxic than the old arsenic-based chemicals that are responsible for the bad reputation of pressure-treated wood. "PT" lumber resists moisture and insect damage, but it is prone to warpage and doesn't take finishes (especially paint) as well as untreated wood.

FEATURED TOOL

Drawknife

To give the edges a natural look, shape them with a drawknife. The drawknife works by pulling it toward your body. You'll need a vise to hold the parts while you're shaping them. Well honed, a drawknife allows you great flexibility. You can hog off large chunks of wood or take very fine shavings. You can buy drawknives at most woodworking stores or in catalogs—generally they are not too expensive.

X-CHAIR CUT LIST

Overall Dimensions: 38" H × 32" D × 11" W

KEY	QTY	PART NAME	DIMENSION	MATERIAL
A	1	Backrest	1½" × 11" × 45"	Douglas fir
B	1	Seat	1½" × 11" × 42"	Douglas fir

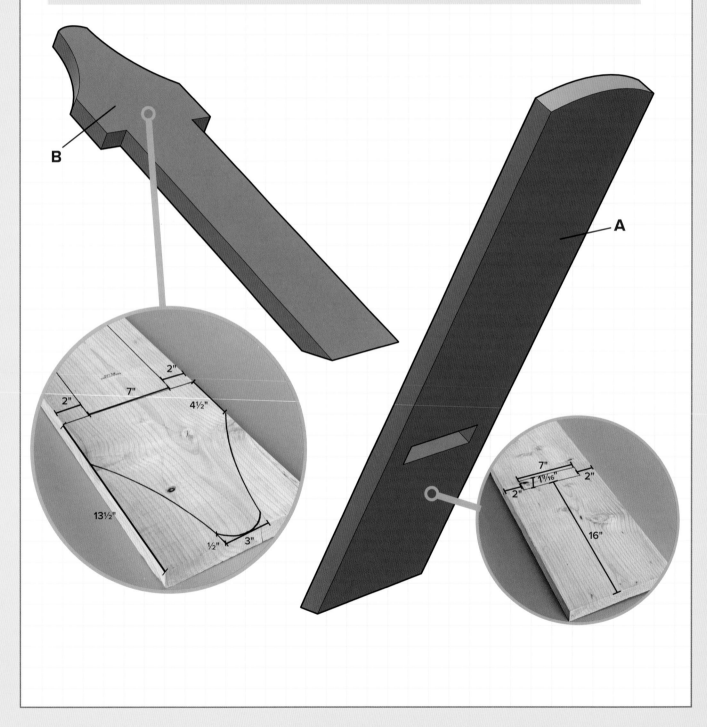

How to Build an X-Chair

STEP 1: Prepare the 8'-long 2 × 12 by rip-cutting about ¼" off of each long edge, using a circular saw and cutting guide (see page 127)—or a table saw if you have one. The finished width of the workpiece should be 11". Removing the beveled factory edges gives the board cleaner lines and makes it look less like a piece of dimensional construction lumber.

STEP 2: Cut the 2 × 12 in half lengthwise, giving you two 48"-long pieces to make the Backrest and the Seat.

STEP 3: Lay out and cut the slot (a kind of mortise) 16" from the end of one board, which will become the Backrest. To cut the slot, drill an access hole (⅜" or so) in each corner, just inside the cutting lines, and cut the opening with a jigsaw. Square off the corners with the jigsaw or a square file.

To cut interior holes and slots, drill out the corners and then connect the dots with a jigsaw to give you straight edges. TIP: The biggest mistake beginners make when using a jigsaw is to apply too much force—this can cause the blade to bend and result in an uneven cut. Just hold the tool firmly and let the saw do the work.

STEP 4: On the Seat board, draw cutting lines 2" from and parallel to the board edges. Mark the cutting lines 13½" from the opposite end of board. These are the stop lines. With a circular saw and straightedge guide, cut along the lines but stop cutting just short of the stop lines. Then, finish the cuts with a handsaw. Make straight shoulder cuts along the stop lines to free the wood waste.

Starter holes

QUICK TIP

Cross-Reference

Make your own straightedge cutting guide and customize it to fit the shoe of your circular saw. This is an invaluable guide, especially if you do no not have access to a table saw for making long, straight cuts. See page 127 for instructions.

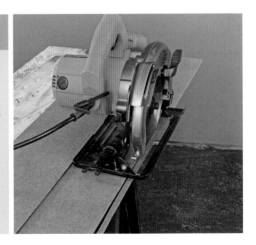

Woodburning Finish

As an alternative to staining, you can achieve a unique appearance using a propane torch. This is a variation on a Japanese wood treatment technique called shou sugi ban. It's supereasy, not to mention mesmerizing and slightly addictive. Make sure you have good ventilation and nothing flammable nearby. Lightly pass the torch flame across the wood surfaces. When you're done burning, let the wood cool, wipe off or sand off any excess charring, and apply a protective finish of your choice.

Just wave the flame over the wood until the desired color is achieved.

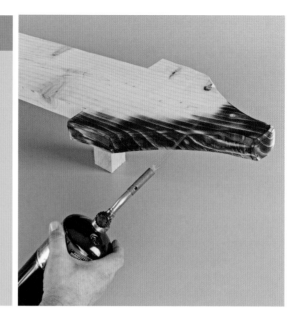

STEP 5: Test the fit of the trimmed end of the Seat board by sliding it into the slot in the Backrest. If the fit is too snug, enlarge the slot slightly by sanding or filing.

STEP 6: Lay out the profile cuts on the sitting end of the Seat board. You'll find the dimensions I used on page 18. These are noncritical dimensions, meaning they won't affect the structural integrity of the chair. But they will affect the appearance and the comfort. Everyone who has tested the chair I built has found this seat shape to be comfortable, but if you are so inclined, you can try out a few different shapes and proportions on some scrap wood. TIP: Use a paint can or other round object with a diameter close to the one you are plotting as a guide for laying out the curved cuts.

STEP 7: Use a jigsaw to cut the seat to the shape you have plotted. Sand the edges smooth.

STEP 8: Now you can make adjustments to the angle of the back and the seat height to suit you. Start by fitting the two parts together so the Seat board is snug in the slot and fully seated against the Backrest. Take a seat and see how it feels.

STEP 9: To make adjustments, trim the front leg (the bottom of the Backrest) and the back leg (the bottom of the Seat board) a little at a time. You'll also want to cut your trim lines so the angle allows the legs to sit flush on a flat surface. The best way to assure good results with this type of cut is to transfer cutting lines using physical aides (as opposed to setting a prescribed cutting angle and hoping it works). In this case, a suitable aide is just a couple of pieces of ¾"-thick scrap wood that raise your pencil high enough to cover both edges of the workpiece.

To physically scribe cutting lines, stack some pieces of scrap wood next to the workpiece until the stack is higher than the top of the workpiece end. Then simply trace around the workpiece, sliding the stack as you go.

STEP 10: Make the angled cuts at the bottoms of the legs. A woodworker with a bandsaw would probably use that tool for this cut, but you can get good results making a careful cut with an ordinary handsaw. Cut both legs and test-sit on the chair. You can make the back more upright by shortening the front leg. Make the back more reclined by shortening the back leg.

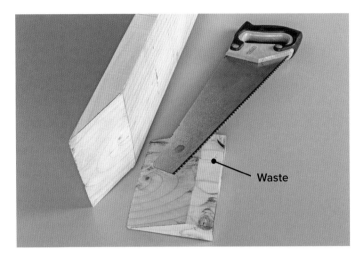

Waste

The angle on the back leg will likely be too steep for your circular saw, so use a handsaw to make this cut.

STEP 11: Give your chair a more finished appearance by tooling a gentle profile into the top end of the Backrest. As shown, we simply cut a curved profile that starts 2" down from each top corner and slopes up evenly to the centerpoint. Lay out the curve and cut it with a jigsaw. Use a sander to smooth all surfaces of both parts.

QUICK TIP

Get yourself a drum sander attachment for your electric or cordless drill and use it to smooth the edges of the curved cuts. If you have access to a drill press, mount the drum sander in that tool to get perfect vertical edges.

STEP 12: Apply the finishing touches. You have many options here. You can simply sand the surfaces and edges and then paint or stain and topcoat the boards. Nothing wrong with that. Since this is such a simple project, I decided to get a little fancy with the finish. I contoured the edges with an old-fashioned tool called a draw knife (see page 17) and then scorched them with a torch to give them some color and interest (see the Featured Skill on page 20).

If you will be taking advantage of the portability of this chair, make a **carrying strap** or some kind of rig to wrap around the two boards for ease of transport (see the photo on page 16).

Nesting Crates

**Leave them rough for the garage, or finish them and stack them together in the living room.
Or just use them as crates.**

A set of these nesting-crate shelves was one of my first woodworking projects. Besides being useful and having a clever design, they're also a great learning project. When I made mine, I just grabbed the cheapest construction-grade boards I could find. That was a mistake. The shelves worked, but these boards weren't very straight to begin with, and they warped further after they dried out. This warping made the flat surfaces not very flat, relegating my shelving project to a life in the garage. So pick straight, flat, and dry "Select" grade lumber for this project.

In building these crates, you'll practice cutting accurate half-lap joinery. With so many identical parts, they're easy to make in multiples. The nesting feature locks them together. A stack of these crates is extra strong if they're stacked staggered like bricks so the gaps are not aligned. If you stack them more than three crates high, make sure to attach them to the wall.

These nesting crates are modular and are held together with a compression fit. They can be arranged in any configuration you choose to form a simple shelving unit. You can offset them, as in the photo on the previous page. Or, make a vertical stack. Just press the slats on the bottom of one crate into the grooves on the top of a lower crate (left) and slide them together until the ends are flush (right) or look however you want them to look.

NESTING CRATES SHOPPING LIST

Wood glue

1½" wood screws

2: 1" × 6" × 96" pine (per crate)

▶ Sandpaper
(120-, 180-, 220-grit)

NESTING CRATE CUT LIST (ONE CRATE)

Overall Dimensions: 13½" H × 10" D × 24" W

KEY	QTY	PART NAME	DIMENSION	MATERIAL
A	4	Frame Top & Bottom	¾" × 2" × 10"	Pine
B	4	Frame Front & Back	¾" × 2" × 12"	Pine
C	5	Slat	¾" × 2" × 24"	Pine

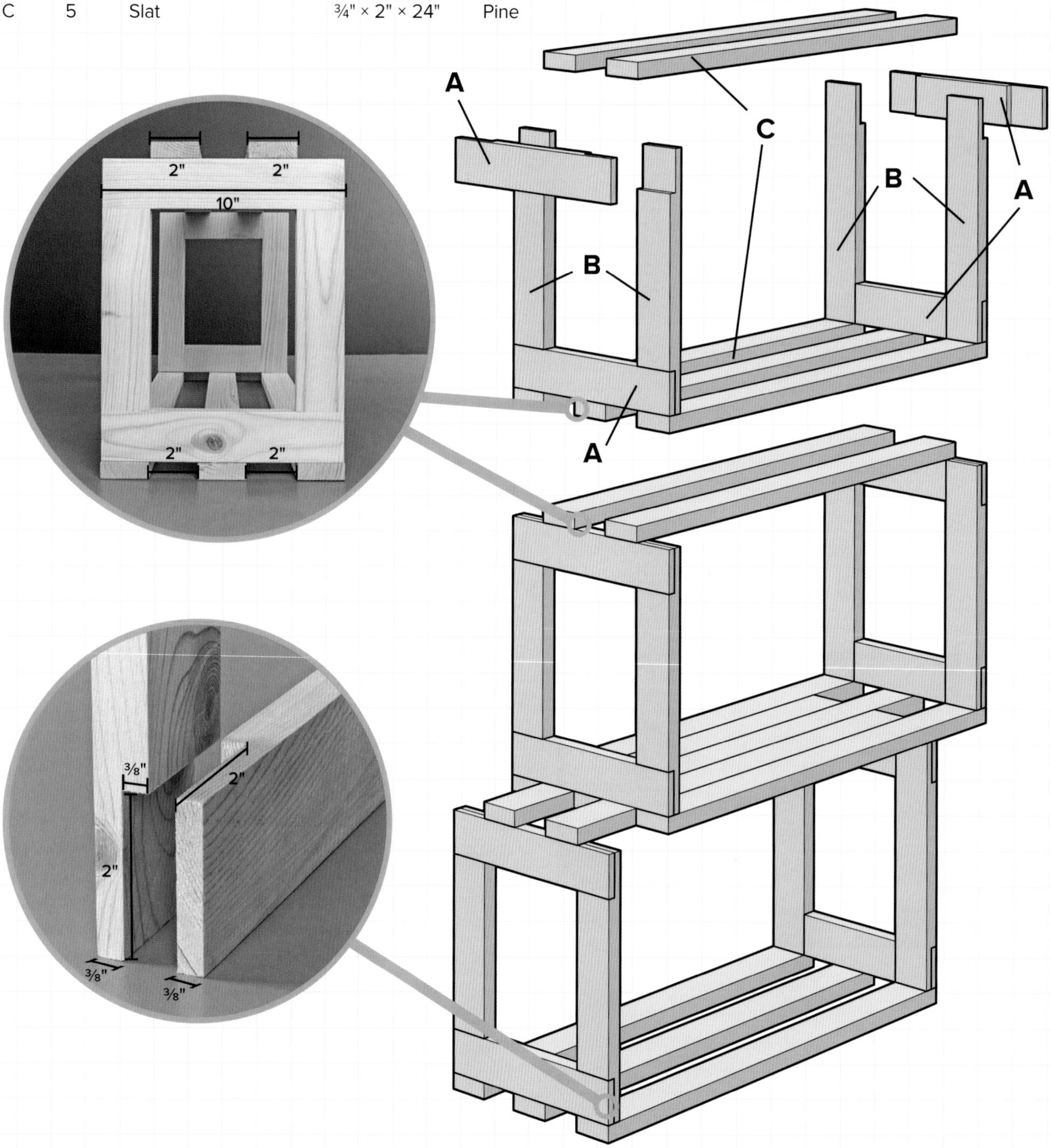

How to Build Nesting Crates

STEP 1: Prepare the 1 × 6 stock by ripping each board into 2"-wide strips. Because the actual width of a nominal 1 × 6 is 5½", you can get two 2"-wide strips out of each board. Use a table saw if you have one, or use a straightedge guide and a circular saw (see page 127) to rip-cut the stock.

STEP 2: Cut your workpieces to length. Each crate requires thirteen boards, so if you are making more than one or two you should use a stop block on a power miter saw to save time and, more importantly, ensure that the like parts are the exact same length.

Some power miter saws come with an extendable fence that has built-in stops for setting cutting lengths, but you can accomplish the same thing (and manage longer workpieces) by clamping a stop block and auxiliary base to your worktable. The surface of the stop block should be the same height as the saw bed.

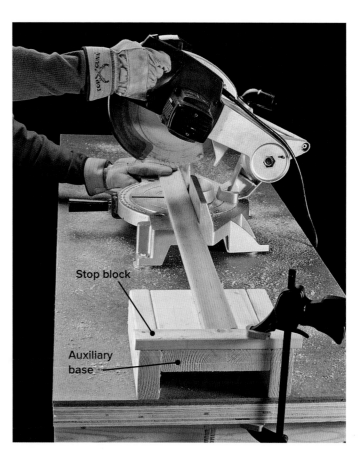

Stop block

Auxiliary base

STEP 3: Make the half-lap joinery cuts. Next to butt joints, half-lap joints are about as simple as joinery gets. Each mating workpiece needs only two cuts: the face cut, which involves cutting parallel to the faces of the board and essentially reducing its thickness; and a shoulder cut, which is the simple trim cut that releases the waste wood from the face cut and is made perpendicular to the board edges. If you own a table saw or a band saw, half-laps are quick and easy. If not, cutting them is a bit more time consuming because you really have to use a handsaw such as a backsaw. It really doesn't matter if you make the face cuts or the shoulder cuts first. I prefer to start with the shoulder cuts so I have a visual stopping point when I make the face cuts on my table saw. Whatever saw you are using, set it up to make a straight cut that is half the thickness of the workpiece. For efficiency, make your shoulder cuts first.

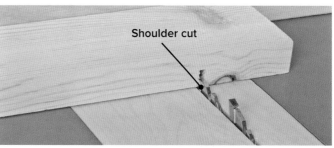

Shoulder cut

Make the shoulder cuts first. I used a tablesaw with a miter gauge and stop block. Another option is to use a hand miter box.

STEP 4: Make the face cuts. These are trickier, even with a table saw. If using a table saw, a tenoning jig is a big help and makes the work much safer (see Featured Tool, next page). If using a handsaw, you'll need to clamp each workpiece vertically into a woodworking vise and carefully cut along a cutting line.

To make the face cuts on a table saw, a tenoning jig is a great help (see next page).

STEP 5: Lightly sand the mating parts in the half-lap joints to get rid of any ridges or splinters.

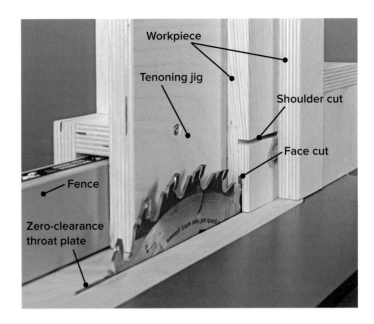

Workpiece

Tenoning jig

Shoulder cut

Face cut

Fence

Zero-clearance throat plate

QUICK TIP

Zero-Clearance Throat Plate

To use a tenoning jig, you'll need a zero-clearance throat plate for your table saw. Most factory throat plates have too much space around the blade, so as you're cutting narrow parts, they can slip down inside the table because there's no surface for them to ride on. A zero-clearance throat plate's opening is just wide enough for the blade to pass through, giving full support to narrow parts.

   To make a zero-clearance throat plate, you'll need material that's the same thickness as your saw's original throat plate. Trace your throat plate onto the blank material, cut it out, and sand to fit. With the blank throat plate in place, set the fence over it to hold it down while you raise the spinning blade through it.

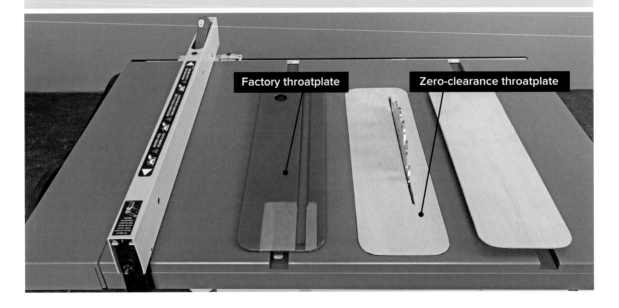

Factory throatplate

Zero-clearance throatplate

STEP 6: Glue the end frames together using spring clamps at the corners. Check to make sure they are square using a carpenter's square or by measuring the diagonals. No additional reinforcement should be needed as there is a lot of glue surface. When the glue is dry, sand the frames.

STEP 7: Predrill clearance holes and countersinks on the faces of the slat ends, centered ⅜" from the board edges. The screws will be covered up when you stack the crates.

STEP 8: Sand all the parts, starting with 100-grit, working your way up to 220-grit.

STEP 9: Clamp each slat to the end frames one at a time so the ends of the slats are flush with the outsides of the frames. Use 2" spacers to set the slat locations. Drill pilot holes into the frames. Fasten the slats using glue and 1½" coarse wood screws or trim-head screws.

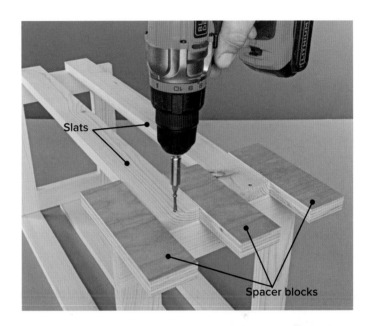

Use spacer blocks to accurately position the slats and hold them in place while you attach them.

STEP 10: Apply a finish of your choice. I chose to keep these crates simple and natural and, because they will live indoors, I did not apply any wood finish.

FEATURED TOOL

Tenoning Jig

A tenoning jig is a staple for any table saw. Cut the tall fence (part A). Cut parts (B) and (C) to fit your saw's fence, and then assemble them as shown. Attach the assembly to the tall fence using glue and screws, and then glue and screw the two vertical fence supports (D) to the back of the fence. Assemble the blade cover box (E) and fasten it to the fence using glue and screws. Attach the back fence (F). Don't glue the back fence; just fasten it with screws. With regular use, the back fence will wear out and need to be replaced. It's critical that the tall fence and back fence are exactly 90° to the saw's top. To use the tenoning jig, clamp your workpiece against the back fence (which you use to push the workpiece through the blade) and to the tall fence. NOTE: You should use a zero-clearance throat plate with this tenoning jig (see previous page).

A tenoning jig offers a safe and accurate option for tooling vertical workpieces on a table saw.

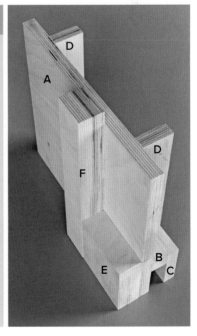

Five Panel Stool

All the elements of a good stool are here: stability, a footrest, and a flat place to sit.

There's no fancy joinery involved here, just a few angled cuts. I used glue and screws to assemble the stool. This stool will look nice with a stain or natural finish, but for me, the addition of bright color on this design really elevates the appeal of the stool. You'll use a circular saw with a cutting guide to cut down the plywood, and learn how to use a router and router template to make the cutouts in the panels.

As I have shown it here, this is largely a router project. Routers are very versatile tools, and if you are at all serious about woodworking, you'll want to look into getting one and learning how to take advantage of the possibilities it will open up for you. But if you are not in a router place yet, an assortment of hand tools (coping saw, files, power jigsaw and sanders) will get the job done, too.

FIVE PANEL STOOL SHOPPING LIST

- ▶ ¾" plywood
- ▶ Trim-head screws or wood screws
- ▶ Sandpaper (120-, 180-, 220-grit)
- ▶ Biscuits for router template (optional)
- ▶ Finishing materials (Primer and enamel paint are used in the project as shown.)

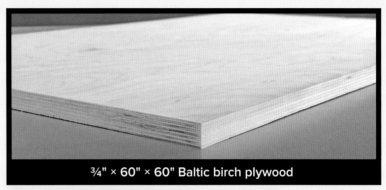

¾" × 60" × 60" Baltic birch plywood

Wood glue

2" stainless-steel or trim-head screws

FEATURED SKILL

Template Routing

To make accurate duplicate parts or cutouts, start by making an accurate router template. Trace the template onto your workpiece, and then rough-cut the pattern, staying just outside the line; up to ¼" is fine. This makes routing easier, as there isn't much material to trim off. If you can fasten the template to a nonvisible surface using finish nails or screws, that's preferable. If not, you'll need to clamp it in place, moving the clamps as you go. When using a router, you'll notice that it wants to pull one direction. Always feed the router against that pull. Use a pattern-following bit with a collar chucked into the router to make the edge profiling cuts.

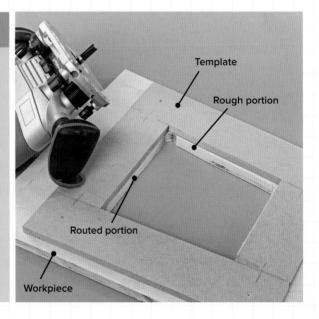

Template

Rough portion

Routed portion

Workpiece

FIVE PANEL STOOL CUT LIST

Overall Dimensions: 24¾" H × 16⅛" D × 16⅛" W

KEY	QTY	PART NAME	DIMENSION	MATERIAL
A	2	Leg	¾" × 16⅛" × 24"	Birch Plywood
B	1	Seat	¾" × 12" × 12"	Birch Plywood
C	1	Top Stretcher	¾" × 10" × 13" *	Birch Plywood
D	1	Bottom Stretcher	¾" × 4" × 15" *	Birch Plywood
*	Cut to fit			

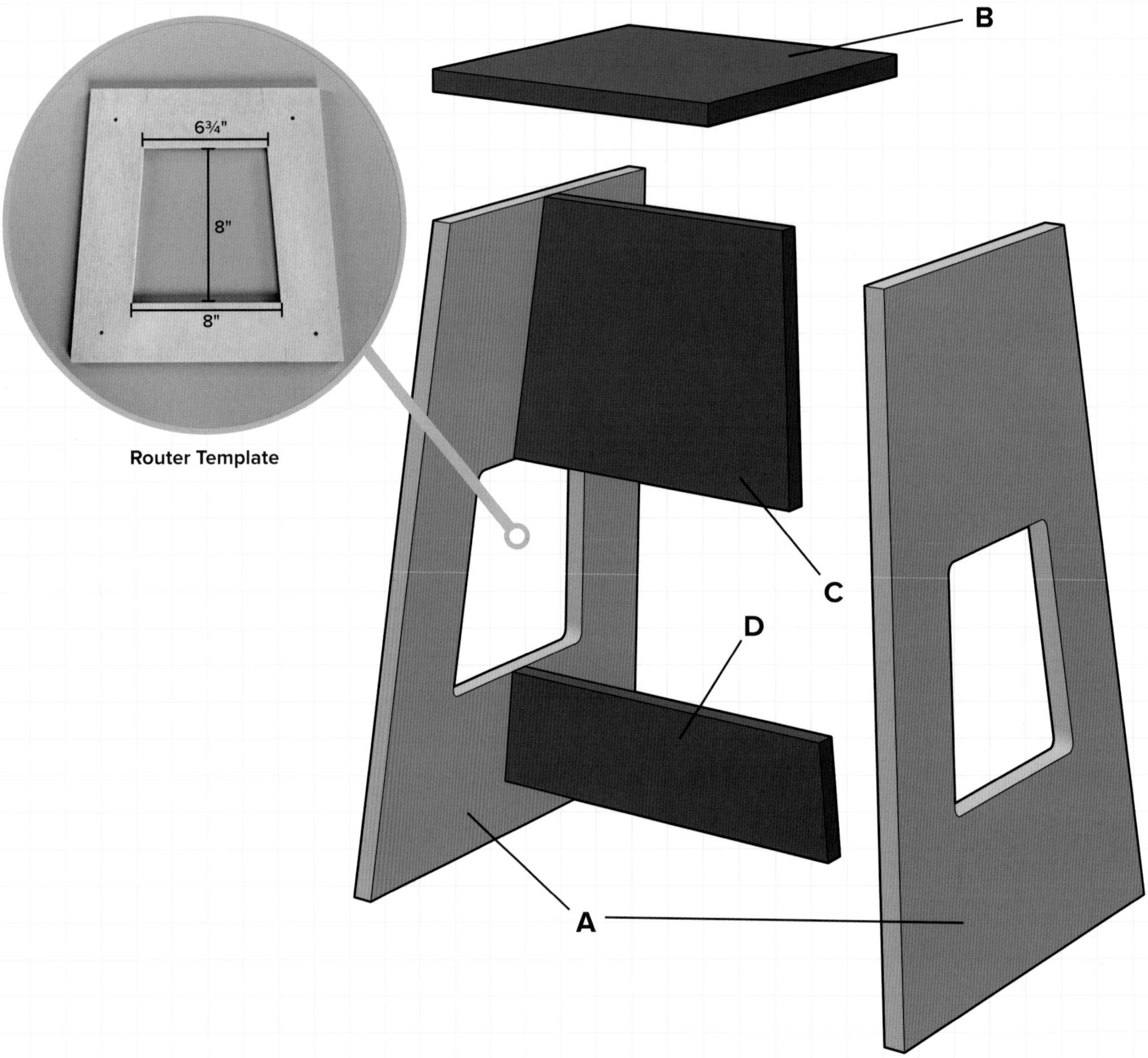
6¾"
8"
8"
Router Template
B
C
D
A

How to Build a Five Panel Stool

STEP 1: Cut the two "blanks" for the legs to rough size, starting out with rectangles that are a few inches longer and wider than the finished length and width of the legs. When making fairly precise parts, it is usually a good idea to cut your workpieces down to a manageable size, rather than trying to manipulate large sheet goods.

STEP 2: Stack the two rectangles and clamp them together for gang-cutting (cutting multiple pieces at the same time for efficiency and to ensure that the cuts are identical). Make the angled cuts along the sides using a circular saw and straightedge cutting guide (see page 127), trimming the workpieces to finished width and taper. For most sheet goods (like plywood or MDF), a blade with a high tooth-per-inch count will give a smoother cut with less blade tear-out.

STEP 3: Cut the legs to length, making parallel 5° bevel cuts along the tops and bottoms. Use a table saw or a circular saw set to 5° and a straightedge to make the bevel cuts.

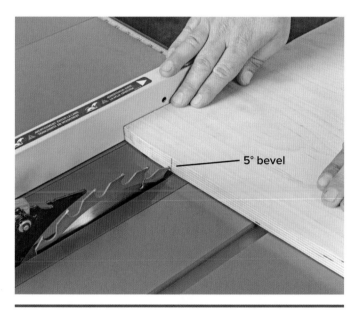

5° bevel

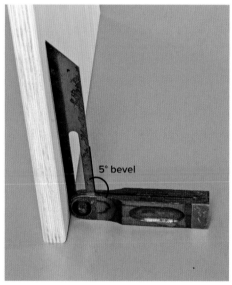

5° bevel

A table saw is well-equipped for making beveled crosscuts in plywood or any other sheet good. If you are using the fence for guidance (instead of a miter gauge), make sure to flip the workpieces after cutting the first end so the bevel of the other end is parallel to the first cut. Check the bevel angles with a T-bevel after both legs are cut.

After making the bevel cuts, set one of the workpieces on a flat surface and set a T-bevel to match the angle of the workpiece relative to the worksurface. Use the T-bevel to check the other legs (top and bottom) to transfer the angle to the stretchers.

STEP 4: If you are using a router and pattern-following bit, make the pattern. Cut 3"-wide strips of ½"-thick plywood to make the four parts of the frame template. Assemble the strips into the template using glue and a biscuit joiner and biscuits.

STEP 5: Position the template on each leg, trace the opening, and then make a rough cutout of the waste, about ¼" inside each cutting line, using a jigsaw (drill starter holes at the corners first). A router and pattern-following bit will give you a smooth finished cut, but they work best if you have removed most of the waste first. If you will rely on a sander or file to finish and smooth the cutouts, you can cut a little closer to the lines with the jigsaw.

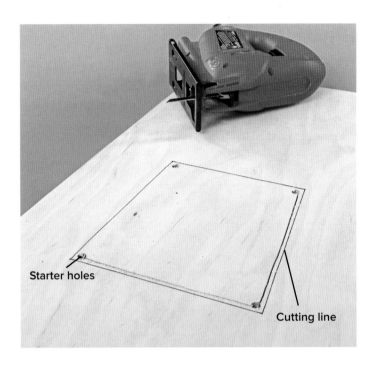

Starter holes

Cutting line

Stay about ¼" outside of the line when you're cutting out the opening. This leaves very little to rout off, and you're far enough away from the line so you don't have to worry about cutting inside of it.

STEP 6: Attach the template to the inside face of each leg and rout the opening using a collared pattern-following bit (see page 29). If you are not using a router, sand the interior cutouts up to the cutting lines with a random-orbit sander.

STEP 7: Rough-cut the seat blank so it is slightly wider all around than the finished size. For a perfectly flush fit, plan on attaching an oversized seat and then sanding it to final size.

STEP 8: Cut the stretchers to final size. Mark the stretcher positions on each leg, and then drill clearance holes for attaching them to the legs.

STEP 9: Attach the stretchers to the legs using glue and wood screws.

To install the stretchers, clamp the top stretcher between the two legs and drill a pilot hole into the stretcher from the top hole on each leg. Remove the clamps, apply glue, and then assemble with screws. Drill pilot holes and install the rest of the screws. Repeat the process for the bottom stretcher.

STEP 10: Test-fit the seat blank onto the stool leg assembly. It should be just slightly oversized on all sides. If it is more than ⅛" or so longer or wider, trim it down with your table saw or circular saw set to a 5° bevel. Attach the seat blank to the tops of the legs with glue and finish nails.

STEP 11: Use power sanders to trim the edges of the seat so they are exactly flush with the lines of the legs and follow the same taper angles (5°). Start with a belt sander, but stop just before you have sanded the edges to flush and finish the shaping with a random orbit sander.

Cut the seat slightly oversize on all sides and then sand it until it is precisely flush once you have attached it.

STEP 12: Sand all the wood surfaces. Wipe clean with a rag and mineral spirits. Apply the finish. If you are using a two-tone paint scheme like I did, prime the entire project first and then tape off the parts that will have the darker paint with masking tape. Apply one or two coats of the lighter color and then remove the tape. Then, tape off the painted surfaces and apply the darker color.

Split-Top Coffee Table

Convert an engineered structural beam into an extraordinary addition to any home.

A low profile and clean lines lend a quiet, comfortable feel to this contemporary coffee table. Construction couldn't be easier. The two top slabs register onto dowels in the tops of the legs, so the entire project has just four parts. This is a very basic design technique that can be adapted to just about any tabletop you want to use: a large wood slab, exotic deck boards, part of an old door... basically, anything that is broad and flat will work. I used an engineered wood beam, which is typically used in rough construction to support interior load. The one I used, called an "LVL" beam (which stands for laminated veneer lumber), is 11½" wide and has up to twice the load-bearing capability of 2 × 12 boards ganged together face-to-face, so I know it will be a durable table. It also has a very interesting grain figure once you do a little sanding. Although it is a strong and visually interesting material, LVL costs around four times as much as dimensional pine lumber, so be prepared for a little sticker shock if you choose it.

SPLIT-TOP COFFEE TABLE SHOPPING LIST

1: 1¾" × 12" (nominal) × 14' LVL beam

Wood glue

Sandpaper (120-, 180-grit)

⅜" dowels or dowel pins*

Wood finish

*DOWEL PINS are sized to be the same diameter as dowels, but they are intended for use only in wood joinery. They are usually made from denser, stronger hardwood than the pine that most dowels are milled from, so they will resist breaking better. And because they are fluted, they allow glue into the dowel hole to create a better, stronger bond than a regular dowel, which will tend to force all the glue down into the bottom of the dowel hole when you drive it in. Many building centers and lumberyards will carry dowel pins, but you may need to look at a woodworking specialty store or online.

QUICK TIP

Sanding Blocks

Most people make hand sanding blocks from pieces of scrap wood and sheets of sandpaper. I prefer to use sanding belts made for a belt sander. Because they are a contiguous loop, you don't have to worry about tucking the ends of the paper around the board, where they usually come off. I just look around the shop and try to find some MDF (see page 41) or plywood scrap and then cut it so it fits snugly inside the belt. You can leave the ends and corners of the board square if you like, but I prefer to round them over. You'll need to experiment a bit to get the length right for the belts you have. You can also custom-cut sanding belts to match the size of your block or the object you are sanding.

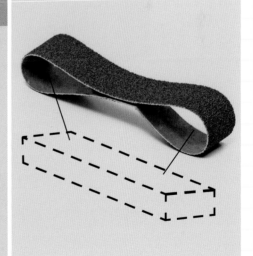

SPILT-TOP COFFEE TABLE CUT LIST

Overall Dimensions: 10¾" H × 24" D × 60" W

KEY	QTY	PART NAME	DIMENSION	MATERIAL
A	2	Top	1¾" × 11½" × 60"	LVL Beam
B	2	Leg	1¾" × 10" × 18"	LVL Beam

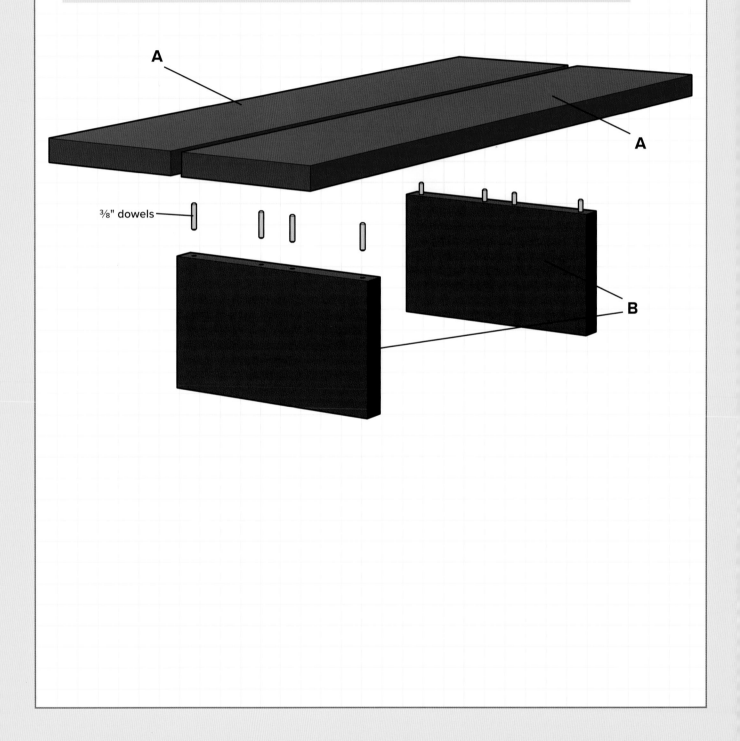

How to Build a Split-Top Coffee Table

STEP 1: Cut two tabletop boards and two legs to length by crosscutting the wood stock. If you are following this plan, you'll need a pair of full-width, 60"-long pieces for the tabletop, as well as two leg parts.

STEP 2: Cut the legs to width: they are narrower in width than the tabletop workpieces. You can either trim 1½" off one edge of each leg, or trim ¾" off each edge. Many woodworkers (myself included) would opt to trim both edges because you never know for sure if the factory edges are actually straight, and sometimes they get dinged up in transit.

STEP 3: Sand the surfaces and edges of all parts up to 180-grit, being careful not to round over any corners; keep everything as square and sharp as possible. Because engineered beams like the ones I used here often have paint and other markings on the surfaces, I started with a belt sander and a 60-grit belt and basically resurfaced them to erase all of the markings. Use a finer belt or a random-orbit sander to finish-sand the surfaces and remove any splinters.

A belt-sander with a 60-grit belt will make quick work of "erasing" paint and lumber markings on any wood workpiece. Run a 2' or longer level across the wood surface to identify any high spots, and then sand them down to be flush with the surrounding surface.

STEP 4: Lay the two tabletop boards upside down on a flat, protected surface. Insert a few ½" spacers between the inner board edges (or if your planned gap differs, use a different spacer width). You can clamp the boards together for marking if you wish, although if you are using engineered beam sections like these, you will find they are rather heavy and not likely to shift. Position the legs exactly where you want them and then trace around them on the undersides of the tabletop pieces.

Position the legs on the underside of the tabletop boards and trace around them. This gives you an exact location when you're locating and drilling the dowel holes in the tops.

STEP 5: Plot out the locations of the dowel joints on the tops of the legs, centered side to side. For this project, I used two dowels per tabletop board at each leg, with a dowel placed 1" in from each end of each leg. You can use more if you wish, but realize that the more dowels you add the harder it becomes to get the dowels all to register in the mating dowel holes during assembly.

STEP 6: Drill the dowel holes in the tops of the legs, slightly deeper than one-half the length of your dowels or dowel pins. The dowel holes should be the same diameter as the dowels (⅜" as shown). If you have a portable drill strand for your power drill, this would be a great time to use it to ensure that the dowel holes are exactly perpendicular to the wood surface you are drilling into.

STEP 7: To transfer the exact locations of the dowel holes in the legs to the undersides of your tabletop pieces, insert dowel centers into the dowel holes in the legs and then press the legs down onto the tabletop inside the outline you drew.

Dowel centers are small metal marking aids that have sharp points in the center. They are sized to match common dowel diameters. Set one dowel center in each hole on the top of each leg so the point is sticking out slightly from the leg. Position the workpiece with the dowel centers against the mating workpiece and press them together. When you separate the workpieces, you will find small drilling points in each tabletop piece at precisely the locations of the dowel holes in the legs.

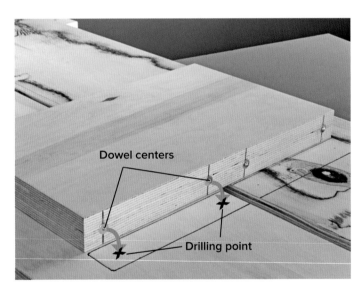

Dowel centers

Drilling point

STEP 8: Separate the legs and tabletop and then apply wood glue into all dowel holes. Drive a dowel pin or dowel into each dowel hole in each leg, and then position the legs over the leg location and seat the other ends of the dowels in the mating dowel holes. Apply some glue to the mating surfaces of the leg and tabletop as well. Rap the bottoms of the legs with a wood mallet to make sure the parts are flush together—but don't get carried away and damage the legs. Remove any glue squeeze-out from each dowel joint before it dries.

STEP 9: Lightly finish-sand all the parts again and then apply the finish. I used a purple mahogany, semitransparent wood stain on the tabletop and a dark walnut stain on the base, followed by a topcoat of low-gloss polyurethane varnish.

Tabletop Options

The basic tablemaking technique shown here is really quite simple and can be adapted pretty easily to just about any tabletop material you like. For example, a beautiful slab of wood or even a section of an old door. As long as the surfaces of the top material are relatively flat, you can use the same doweling technique shown in this split-top project to affix the top to the legs. And even if the underside of the workpiece you want to use for the top is not flat and even, you can always scribe the tops of the legs to follow the surface profile. It makes positioning the dowels a bit trickier, but if you use the dowel centers as shown in step 7, you should get good results.

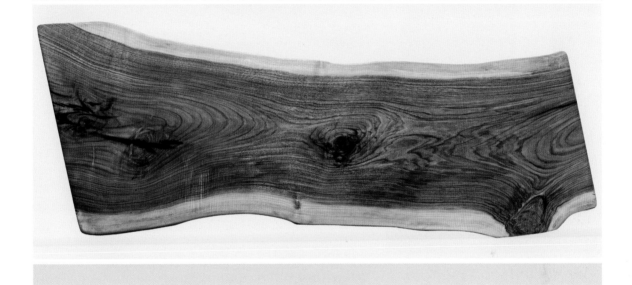

Knockdown Workbench

Build a rock-solid bench that folds up and stores flat against the wall.

A large, sturdy workbench is a necessity when building projects. But good-quality benches are very expensive, and not everyone has room for one. This workbench solves both problems. I used three layers of ¾" MDF for the top; it's flat, smooth, and exceptionally stable, and it provides plenty of heft—read, it is superheavy. The framework is made with ordinary construction lumber. The unique knockdown (KD) pipe-and-bolt joinery system creates some of the sturdiest joints I've used. Butt hinges recessed into the top stretchers of the legs provide the fold-up action, but they're optional. You could fasten the top with screws if storability is not important for you.

KNOCKDOWN WORKBENCH SHOPPING LIST

1: ¾" × 16" copper tubing

8: ⁵⁄₁₆" × 4" hex bolts

8: ⁵⁄₁₆" hex nuts

8: ⁵⁄₁₆" flat washers

2: 2" × 4" × 96" pine

2: 2" × 6" × 96" pine

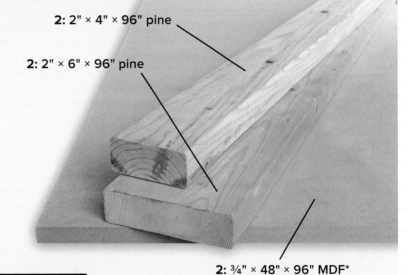

2½" wood screws

2: ¾" × 48" × 96" MDF*

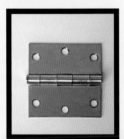

4: 3" butt hinges

Wood glue

*MDF stands for *medium-density fiberboard*. It is a very dense and heavy sheet stock used mostly for horizontal surfaces and underlayment. It has a flat, smooth surface and good dimensional stability that make it an excellent choice for painting or veneering—a related product called MDO (medium-density overlay) is even better for painting because it has a very smooth paintable paper covering on the surfaces. MDF is not designed for structural use in situations where it will get torque and side pressure, as with sheathing. Plywood or oriented strand board (OSB) are better.

KNOCKDOWN WORKBENCH CUT LIST

Overall Dimensions: 34" H x 23½" D x 72" W

KEY	QTY	PART NAME	DIMENSION	MATERIAL
A	4	Leg	1½" × 3½" × 31¾"	Pine
B	4	Short Stretcher	1½" × 5½" × 23½"	Pine
C	2	Long Stretcher	1½" × 5½" × 63½"	Pine
D	3	Top	¾" × 23½" × 72"	MDF

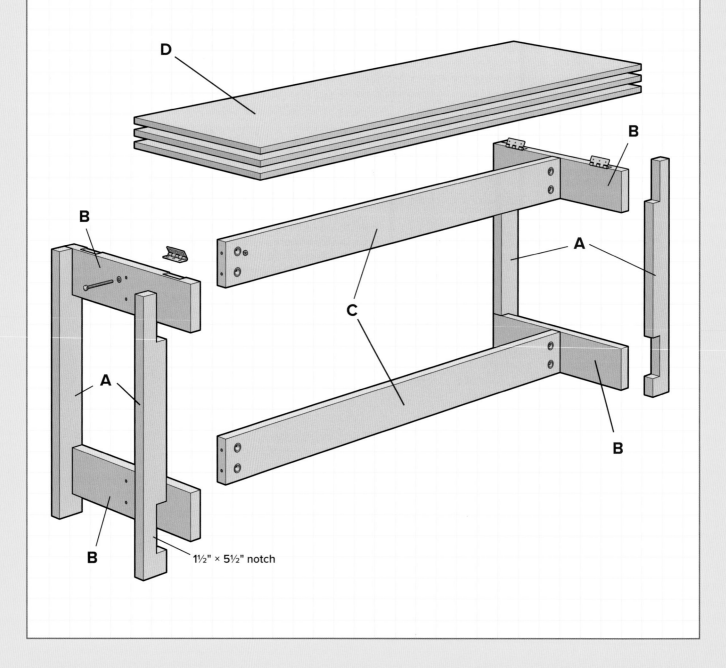

1½" × 5½" notch

How to Build a Knockdown Workbench

STEP 1: Cut the 2 x 4 legs and the 2 x 6 stretchers to length.

STEP 2: Cut a 1½" deep by 5½" long notch at the top of each leg for the 2 x 6 stretchers at the tops (the top of the stretcher will be flush with the leg tops). A jigsaw is a good tool for these cuts; or, you can make multiple passes across ganged workpieces with a circular saw and then clean up the kerf marks with a wood chisel. Then, on the same edges as the first notches, cut 1½ x 5½" notches for the bottom stretchers, 2½" up from the bottoms of the legs.

STEP 3: Prepare the long and short stretchers for the knockdown joints. Plot out the locations for the ⅞"-diameter guide holes that will house the copper tubing "barrels" in the joint. The center points of the guide holes should be 1½" from the top and bottom edges of the long stretches, and 2" in from the ends. Drill the ⅞" guide holes (a multispur drill bit will limit tear-out, but use a backer board, too).

STEP 4: On a flat surface, position the short stretchers next to the long stretchers and transfer the centerpoints of the tubing holes to the inside faces of the short stretchers. Drill ⅜"-diameter bolt guide holes through the faces of the short stretchers and into the ends of the long stretchers. Clamp or tack the parts together before drilling. Drill until you have cleared the tubing holes.

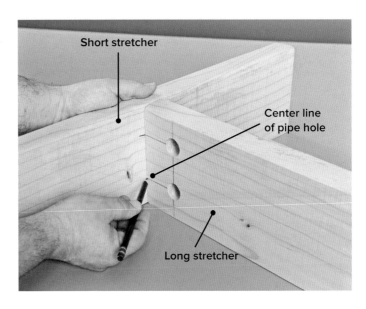

> **Transfer the pipe layout lines to the short stretchers, directly from the long stretchers, so the holes line up perfectly.**

STEP 5: Cut the 1½"-long copper pipe sections from ¾" copper tubing. A tubing cutter will give a nice clean cut. Deburr the cuts with emery paper if necessary and tap them into the holes using a nonmarring mallet. The copper tubes should fit snugly, creating a friction fit.

STEP 6: Extend the ⅜"-diameter bolt guide holes into the outer wall of each copper tube barrel. Do not drill into the other side of the tube.

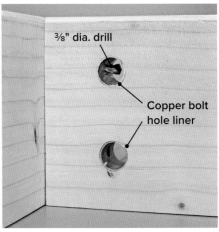

> **When you drill the stretcher clearance holes, drill only through one wall of the copper pipe.**

STEP 7: Insert a ⁵⁄₁₆" × 4" hex bolt and washer into each knockdown hole. Reach into the copper tubes and attach a nut to each bolt. Hand-tighten the nuts and then tighten the hex bolts to draw the parts together.

The knockdown joints have copper tube-lined clearance holes so you can attach a nut to each bolt end and also reach in to loosen the nut when you want to knock down the workbench for storage or transfer.

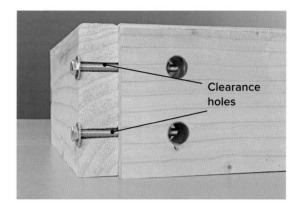

Clearance holes

STEP 8: Fit the short stretchers into the notches you cut into the legs to make the workbench base assembly. Fasten the stretchers to the legs with 2½" wood screws driven through the inside face of the stretchers and into legs, through the notches.

When you attach the hinges, make sure they'll fold up in the right direction.

STEP 9: Cut the bench top pieces slightly oversize from MDF. Glue and screw two of the pieces together face-to-face on a flat surface. Attach the top (third) layer to the bottom layers using countersunk screws, without glue, driven up through the bottom. This way, there are no screw heads on the worksurface, and you can easily replace the top when it gets beat up from use.

STEP 10: Trim the assembled top to finished size using a circular saw and a cutting guide (see page 127).

STEP 11: Cut mortises for the hinge plates with a wood chisel as needed to get the legs to clear properly. Turn the top upside down and center the assembled base on it. Mark the leg and hinge locations on the underside of the top, and then disassemble the base. Attach the legs to the underside of the top using the hinges.

Add a bench vise (below) or woodworking vise to your workbench. Many vises are easy to remove when you wish.

QUICK TIP

To disassemble the workbench for storage or transport, remove the knockdown bolts holding the stretchers together and then simply fold the legs up.

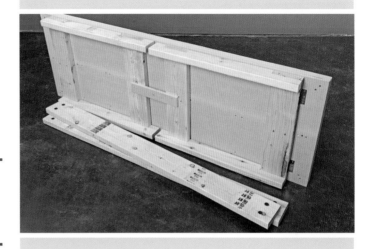

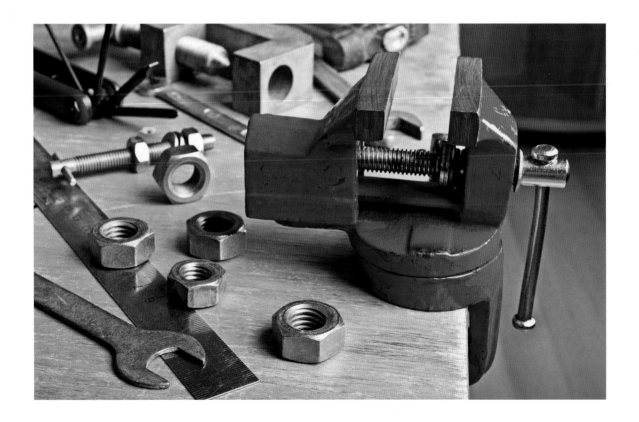

Hall Table

This slim table can nestle into a hallway, entryway or behind a sofa for efficient storage and display.

This slender table is built using standard 2 × 4s for legs and one premade, edge-glued spruce board for the shelves. By downsizing the 2 × 4s just a bit, they'll lose their rounded corners. This helps them look less like construction lumber. Pick through the pile to get the best-looking, straightest boards you can find.

HALL TABLE SHOPPING LIST

2: 2" × 4" × 96" pine*

1: 1" × 12" × 48" pine

*SELECTING LUMBER:
When you're picking through a lumber pile, consider the relative weight of each board. Some might be really heavy compared to others. A heavy board likely means that it still has a high moisture content; it may even feel wet to the touch. These boards are kiln dried, but sometimes they sit outside and get soaked in the rain. Avoid these boards. As they dry out, they may twist and warp, making them unsuitable for building furniture (not to mention dangerous to cut).

Sandpaper (120-, 180-grit)

Forged nails

Wood glue

Wood stain

Wood finish

FEATURED HARDWARE

Forged Nails

Unfortunately, you won't be able to find these at home centers. Instead, you'll need to harness your mule and drive your trap to the village smithy. Or just hop on the Internet. On this project, I'm relying on glue to hold these joints; the nails are mainly decorative, but they do add a measure of mechanical strength. If you can find an actual blacksmith near where you live to make the nails for you, see if he or she will let you watch. It's fascinating!

HALL TABLE CUT LIST

Overall Dimensions: 35" H × 12" D × 48" W

KEY	QTY	PART NAME	DIMENSION	MATERIAL
A	4	Leg	1½" × 3" × 35"	Pine
B	1	Shelf	1" × 12" × 43"	Spruce
C	1	Top	1" × 12" × 48"	Spruce

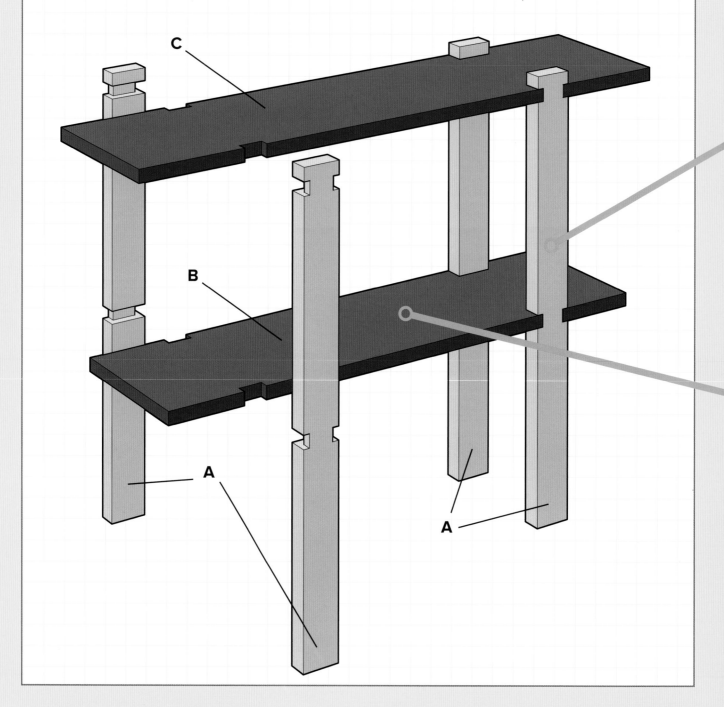

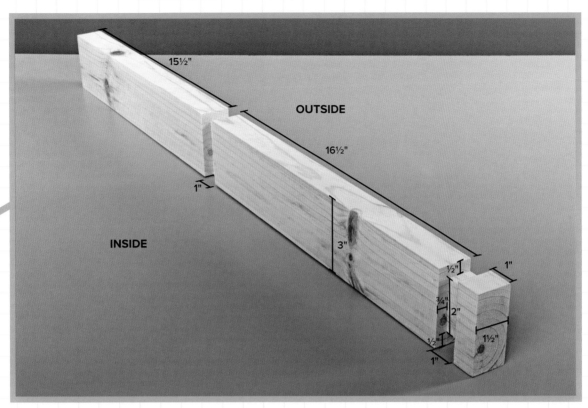

The Hall Table legs require some tooling, but the net result is that the notches you cut into them create cozy homes for the shelving and add a lot of stability to the otherwise narrow and potentially spindly furnishing.

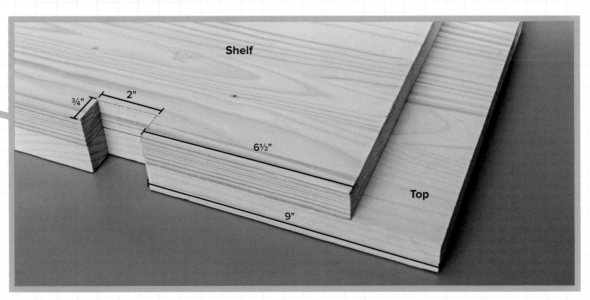

The Hall Table shelves are notched to fit into the notches on the legs, a little like the Lincoln Logs many of us payed with as kids. To make sure the shelf notches are identical in size, gang the shelves together and cut the notches at the same time.

How to Build a Hall Table

STEP 1: Cut the shelf and top to length. The shelf is 5" shorter than the top, so there will be a 2½" overhang from the top to the shelf on each end. The material I used for these parts is a premade edge-glued board that is a full 12" wide and a full (not nominal) 1" thick. Engineered boards like this tend to have more dimensional stability than a nominal pine 1 x 12 would, so they warp and twist less. But you can certainly use a 1 × 12 if you wish, just be sure to adjust the notch thicknesses down to ¾".

STEP 2: Place the shelf board on top of the tabletop board so the overhang is equal (2½") at each end and the edges are flush. Clamp the boards together. Lay out the notches in the board edges according to the dimensions on page 49, using a speed square or try square to make notch cutting lines.

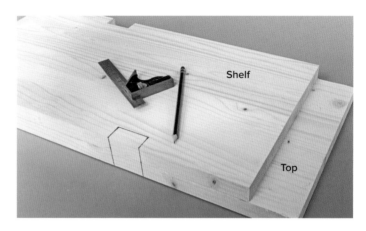

Clamp the top and shelf together and lay out the notches at the same time.

STEP 3: Cut the notches into the top and shelf edges. You can use a handsaw (look for one called a "gentleman's saw") or even a jigsaw to cut them. But if you have access to a table saw and a dado blade set (see page 51), this would be a great time to use them.

STEP 4: Sand the top and shelf, working your way up to 220-grit. Break over the sharp edges as well.

STEP 5: Cut the legs to length from 2 × 4 stock. I also trimmed the stock down in width, taking ¼" off each for a finished width of 3". A table saw is perfect for this job, but you can use a circular saw and straightedge guide instead, or even a router table.

STEP 6: Lay out the notches in the legs according to the dimensions on page 49. Double-check to make sure the thickness of the notches matches the thickness of the shelf and top (exactly 1" with the material I used).

STEP 7: Cut the notches in the legs. See the tip on using dado blade sets on page 51 to cut them on your table saw as I did. Or, gang the legs together and cut the notches by making multiple passes to remove waste between the shoulders with a circular saw.

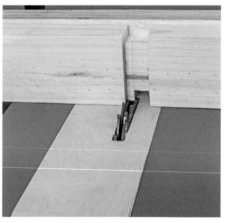

One fast and accurate way to cut notches is to use a double miter gauge and table saw with a dado set. Cut the leg dadoes using a stacked dado set, in combination with a double miter gauge (see page 97) and stop block. Rotate the legs to continue the cut around three sides of each leg. Since the shelves are 1" thick, each dado requires setting the stop block twice.

STEP 8: Sand the legs prior to assembly. Start with 100-grit and work your way up to 220-grit.

STEP 9: Stain the legs next if you'd like them to be a different color than the shelf and top.

STEP 10: Test-fit the shelves and legs and then assemble the table using glue and clamps. When the glue is dry, predrill for the forged nails and then tap them carefully into place. Apply a topcoat finish of your choice.

Drive forged nails using a nonmarring mallet, or place a block of wood on the head as a striking surface. This way you won't ding up the head or expose any raw steel underneath the black, forged patina.

FEATURED SKILL

Stacked Dado Set

A dado blade set is a must-have tool for table saw owners. It allows you to cut any size groove, dado, or rabbet quickly and accurately. Invest in the best quality you can afford. A dado set has two outer blades and a set of "chippers" that go in between the outer blades to make wider cuts. Typically, you can make cuts from ¼" to ¹³⁄₁₆" wide. A good dado set also includes shims to allow dialing in an exact fit. If you own a 10" table saw, particularly if it's a small contractor or portable saw, I recommend a 6" dado set, as opposed to the more common 8" set. Smaller saws just don't have enough power to handle an 8" stacked dado set.

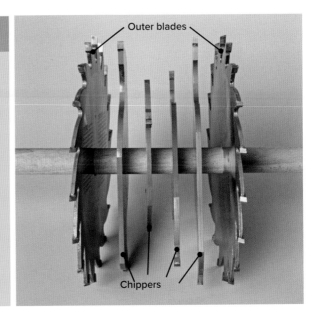

Outer blades

Chippers

Cantilevered Stand

Robust with some industrial flair, use this heavy-duty piece as a TV stand, plant stand, coffee table, or even a seat.

Construction-grade materials (4 × 4 posts and OSB sheathing) and hardware give this stand an industrial look as well as industrial strength. When sanded and finished, oriented strand board (OSB) is quite visually appealing, with minute details on both the top and the edge. You'll have the opportunity to practice some angled half-lap joinery and notch cutting. I'll also go through the often-ignored but very important process of predrilling for screws and bolts. By learning the anatomy of predrilled holes, your screwed joints will be tighter and stronger, and you'll stop splitting boards and stripping or breaking screws.

CANTILEVERED STAND SHOPPING LIST

4: ⁵⁄₁₆" 4" lag screw
& 4: ⁵⁄₁₆" 5" lag screw

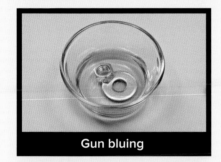

4: ⁵⁄₁₆" hex bolts

Gun bluing

Sandpaper
(120-, 180-, 220-grit)

2: 4" × 4" × 96" fir or pine

1: ¾" × 48" x 96" OSB

4: ⁵⁄₁₆" hex nuts

16: ⁵⁄₁₆" washers

1 ½" wood screws

Wood glue

CANTILEVERED STAND CUT LIST

Overall Dimensions: 23½" H x 31" D x 43½" W

KEY	QTY	PART NAME	DIMENSION	MATERIAL
A	2	Foot	3½" × 3½" × 31"	Fir or Pine
B	4	Leg	3½" × 3½" × 26"	Fir or Pine
C	1	Shelf	1½" × 16" × 34½"	Double Layer OSB
D	1	Top	1½" × 24" × 43½"	Double Layer OSB

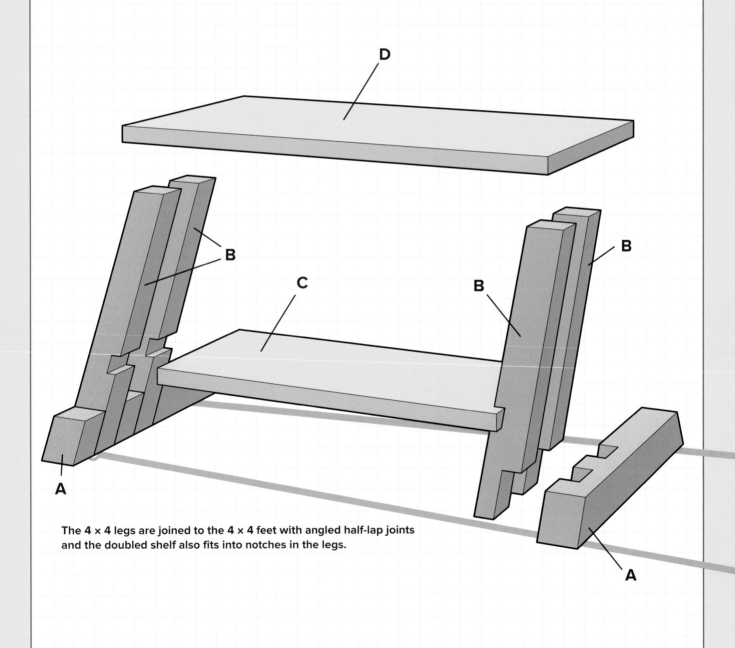

The 4 × 4 legs are joined to the 4 × 4 feet with angled half-lap joints and the doubled shelf also fits into notches in the legs.

How to Build a Cantilevered Stand

STEP 1: Cut the feet to length. The ends of each foot are cut at opposite 60° angles, so they splay outward. You can make these cuts on a table saw very easily, or draw cutting lines and cut with a handsaw.

STEP 2: Lay out the notches for the legs in the sides of the feet. The shoulders of the notches should be parallel to the foot ends (60° angle) and 3½" wide at the top and the bottom to accept the 4 × 4 legs in half-lap joints (so cut them 1¾" deep). The first notch on each foot should start 3½" from the front end of the foot and the second notch for the back leg should be 3½" back from the first notch. A good way to cut the notches is to "hog out" the waste wood in the notch area with multiple passes of a circular saw set to 1¾" cutting depth. Finish with a wood chisel.

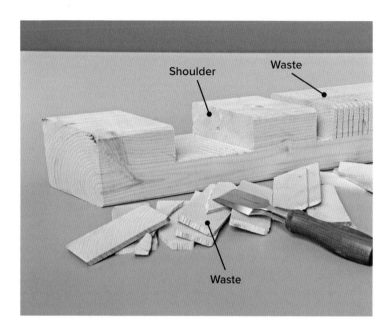

Cut half-lap joints in the feet by cutting accurate shoulders for each notch first. Then make multiple passes through the waste area. Clean out the leftovers using a chisel.

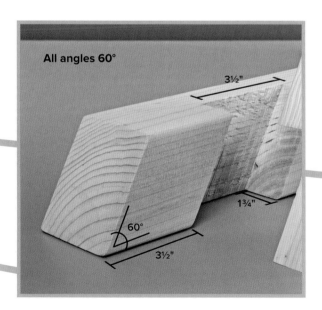

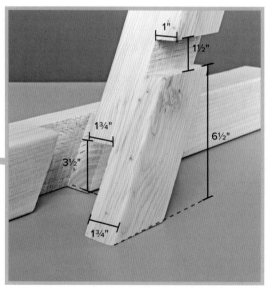

STEP 3: Cut the 4 × 4 legs to length, with the ends angled at 60° to match the leg notches.

STEP 4: Lay out the half-laps and shelf notches on the legs. The half-laps are 1¾" deep and 3½" high, parallel to the angled leg bottoms. Cut these using the same method you used for the feet. The shelf notches should be 1½" high and 1" deep, 6½" up from the leg bottoms and parallel to them.

STEP 5: Cut the shelf and top pieces to rough size, and then face-glue them together using 1½" wood screws, countersunk and driven from the undersides of the workpieces.

Cut the top and shelf to final size with a circular saw and a straightedge cutting guide (see page 127). The front and back edges should follow the same 60° angles as the cuts and notches on the other project parts.

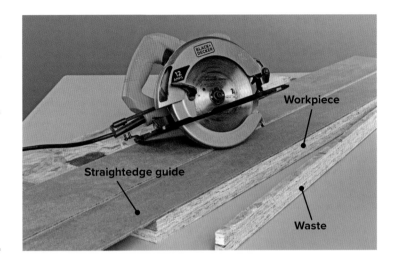

STEP 6: Cut the shelf and top to finished size. Sand them smooth and break over the sharp corners.

STEP 7: OPTIONAL: Permanently color the hardware using gun bluing (see page 95 for more information) before making the fastener-reinforced joints.

STEP 8: Drill guide holes for one lag bolt at each leg/foot half-lap joint. Make the guide holes ⁵⁄₁₆" in dimeter. Attach the legs to the feet with the 5" bolts. You can glue these joints if you wish, but if you may want to disassemble the project someday, leave the glue out—the half-lap joints will be plenty strong.

STEP 9: Position the shelf in its notches and clamp the shelf/leg/foot assembly together. Test-fit the top onto the tops of the legs and lay a straightedge across the front of the top and the shelf to make sure they form a line parallel to the front ends of the legs.

STEP 10: Attach the shelf to the legs by driving one ⁵⁄₁₆ × 4" lag screw at each joint.

STEP 11: Set the top onto the base assembly and shift it around until it is in just the right position. Drill one counterbored lag-screw pilot hole through the top at each leg location, centered on the leg top. The counterbored recesses should be just deep enough to allow the bolt head, including a washer, to be flush with the top surface.

A cordless impact driver makes easy work of driving the lag screws used in this project.

STEP 12: Attach the tops by driving 4" lag screws down into the leg tops. After drilling the counterbore recesses, drill clearance holes for lag bolts the rest of the way through the top. Sand off any layout marks. Apply a protective finish if desired.

FEATURED SKILL

Pilots, Countersinks, and Counterbores

One of the most common mistakes in using screws is not predrilling. Without proper predrilling, the risk of splitting your parts is very high.

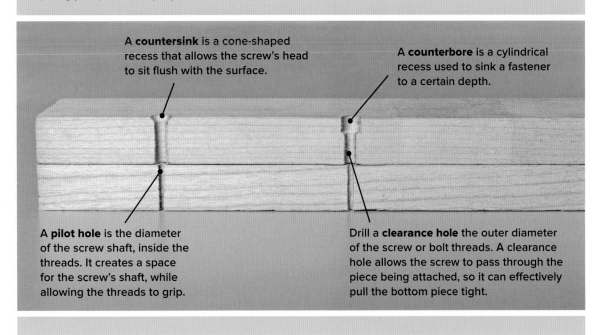

A **countersink** is a cone-shaped recess that allows the screw's head to sit flush with the surface.

A **counterbore** is a cylindrical recess used to sink a fastener to a certain depth.

A **pilot hole** is the diameter of the screw shaft, inside the threads. It creates a space for the screw's shaft, while allowing the threads to grip.

Drill a **clearance hole** the outer diameter of the screw or bolt threads. A clearance hole allows the screw to pass through the piece being attached, so it can effectively pull the bottom piece tight.

Bridle Joint Stool

A rock-solid stool that flaunts the beautiful grain figure of white oak.

A good stool needs to be sturdy. The joints used in this stool—called bridle joints—are similar to mortise-and-tenon joints, except the mortise ends are open. Using a technique called drawboring to pin the joints together, glue isn't necessary, but I use it anyway, just to be on the safe side. The precision joinery may look intimidating, but using a shop-made tenoning jig for the tablesaw makes cutting the joints a simple process. And once you're set up, it's easy to make multiples.

BRIDLE JOINT STOOL SHOPPING LIST

White oak*

Min. 1: 1½" × 1½" stock
(14 lineal feet) or
2: 2" × 2" × 8' (nominal)

1: 1" × 8" (nominal) × 30" long

*HARDWOOD: Some building centers and most lumberyards carry a selection of dimensioned hardwoods that have been milled to a few standard sizes (these are usually designated as "S4S" which stands for "sanded four sides"). In most cases, the species are fairly limited (red oak, maple, perhaps walnut and white oak). If you can find hardwood that has been milled to 2 × 2 and 1 × 8 or 1 × 4 specifications it will simplify this (and many other) projects built from hardwood. For this stool, for example, a couple of 8' 2 × 2s and a 3' length of 1 × 8 (or 6' of 1 × 4) will get you there. If your supplier does not stock white oak in these dimensions, you can switch to another species (red oak is much more common) or purchase just about any hardwood in random widths and thickness and mill the rough stock to finished size yourself. Most lumberyards will custom-mill hardwood to your specs for a fee.

**#10 1½"
wood screws**

▶ **No. 20 biscuits***

*BISCUITS: Biscuits are football-shaped joint reinforcements that fit into slots cut with a biscuit joiner (also called a plate joiner). In this project, they are used to align and strengthen the joint or joints made to edge-glue oak strips to make the stool top. You can get by without them by using dowels at the joints instead, or you may even be fine relying solely on the glue, since the seat is attached to the stool stretchers in multiple locations.

Polyurethane finish

▶ **Sandpaper (100-, 180-, 220-grit)**
▶ **⅜" oak doweling**

BRIDLE JOINT STOOL CUT LIST

Overall Dimensions: 24¾" H × 14" D × 13" W

KEY	QTY	PART NAME	DIMENSION	MATERIAL
A	4	Leg	1½" × 1½" × 24"	White Oak
B	2	Foot Rail	1½" × 1½" × 14"	White Oak
C	3	Stretcher	1½" × 1½" × 13"	White Oak
D	1	Top	¾" × 14" × 13"	White Oak

Bridle joints function very much like mortise-and-tenon joints, except that the "mortise" is at the end of the workpiece and is open so it can slide over the "tenon," which may be cut into the interior of the workpiece or on one end.

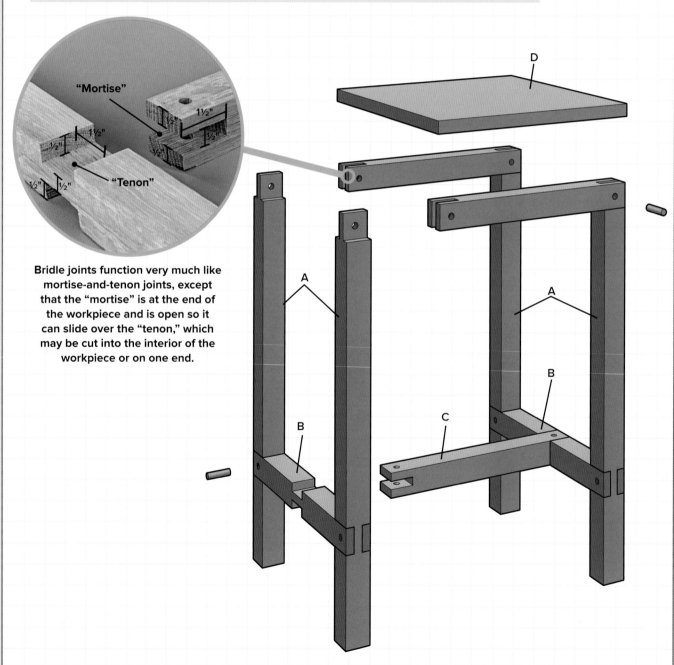

How to Build a Bridle Joint Stool

STEP 1: Prepare your oak stock so the material for the legs, rails, and stretchers is 1½ × 1½" and the material for the stool top is ¾" thick (see note on page 59).

STEP 2: Cut the legs and stretchers to length from the 1½ × 1½" stock. When cutting hardwood, a fine-tooth blade will yield a cleaner cut, but make sure the blade is sharp, or it is likely to burn the wood because the amount of friction and heat generated by cutting hardwoods is greater than it is for softwoods like pine.

STEP 3: Lay out and cut the notches in the legs and foot rails. These are relatively simple cuts because you can keep the workpieces lying on their sides. A table saw with a dado blade set (see page 51) is a perfect tool for these cuts. Or you can remove waste wood with multiple passes of a circular saw and then clean up the notches with a wood chisel.

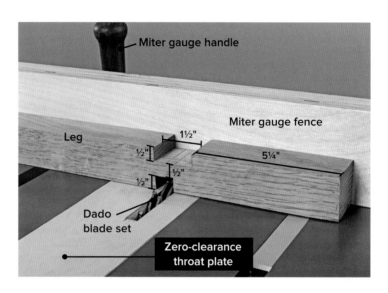

A stacked dado set in conjunction with a miter gauge makes fast work of cutting large notches.

STEP 4: The bridle joints in this project are pegged with oak dowels for reinforcement. Double-check the diameter of your doweling stock before choosing your drill bit for the guide holes. The dowels I used were exactly ⅜" in diameter (I used my calipers to check), so I chose a ⅜" Forstner bit mounted in my drill press to bore the holes. Mark drilling centerpoints at the end of each stretcher, ¾" in from the end and ¾" from each side NOTE: You'll cut the notches in the stretchers after the peg holes are drilled. Drill the guide holes. If you don't have a drill press, mark and drill these pieces from both sides.

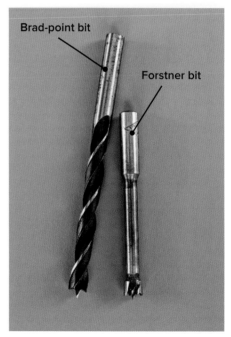

Brad-point bits (left) and Forstner bits (right) are designed to bore holes with clean sides and flat bottoms. Forstner bits are best used in a drill press, as they can throw the drill if the bit wanders out of vertical and jams. Brad-point bits are more forgiving and may be used safely with a hand-held power drill. The center spur on each bit type makes it easy to get the bit started in a precise location.

STEP 5: Cut the open "mortises" in all the ends of the foot rails and all three stretchers. Because the workpiece should be in a vertical position to make these cuts, they are a bit trickier. A tenoning jig and table saw is by far the most accurate and safest way to make these joinery cuts (see page 27). Alternately, you can clamp each workpiece in a vertical position in a bench vise. Drill a ⅜" hole marking the bottom of the mortise. Then carefully cut the mortise cheeks using a hand saw. Square up the notch with a wood chisel.

A table saw and tenoning jig are designed for making cuts like those you'll need to create the notches in the ends of the workpieces. (See the tip on Making Tenoning jigs, page 27).

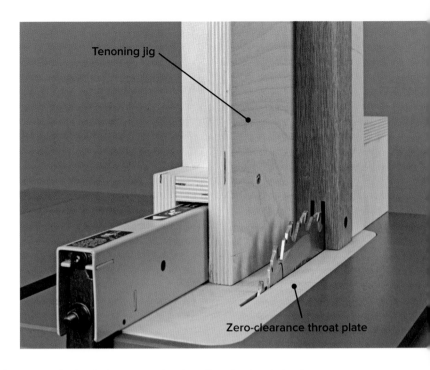

Tenoning jig

Zero-clearance throat plate

STEP 6: I used peg holes that are very slightly offset to pin the bridle joints together (see Drawboring, below). The best way to do this is to mechanically transfer the centerpoint of each peg hole in the outer ("mortise") workpiece to the "tenon." To do this, fit each bridle joint together individually. Insert the drill bit into the hole so the point makes a mark on the tenon of the mating part. Do this for all joints

STEP 7: Disassemble each joint and mark a drilling point on the tenon that is between ⅟₃₂" and ⅟₆₄" closer to the outside end of the joint. Drill the peg hole in the tenon at this adjusted point for all joints.

FEATURED SKILL

Drawboring

Drawboring is a time-tested method of securing two pieces of wood together. The key in drawboring is that the hole in the tenon is offset a bit from the hole in the mortise. Because of this offset, as the peg is driven, it draws the joint together. The offset doesn't need to be more than about ⅟₆₄" in a joint this size, as it exerts a lot of force when the peg is driven. Make sure you offset the new drilling hole in the tenon away from the point where the parts mate—the goal is to draw them together, not force them apart.

After marking the centerpoint of the hole already drilled in the mortise onto the tenon, adjust it by ⅟₆₄" or so toward the outer end of the joint and drill the peg hole in the mortise workpiece.

Original center point

Offset drilling point

QUICK TIP

Put a Point on your Pegs

To make pegging the joint easier and smoother, whittle a point onto one end of a starter peg before driving it with a wood or rubber mallet. Make sure the dowel you are using for the peg is long enough that you will have uncut doweling extending beyond the wood surfaces on both sides of the joint.

STEP 8: Apply wood glue to both mating parts for each bridle joint, then slide the tenon member into the mating mortise. Drive the starter peg followed by the final peg all the way through the joint so the tips of the peg extend past the wood surfaces on both sides. Wipe off excess glue squeeze-out.

STEP 9: To assemble the stool base, repeat the pegging process on each foot rail to leg joint, followed by the lower stretcher and finishing with the bridle joints at the top stretchers.

Peg (or "pin") the bridle joints with dowels. Use an unsharpened piece of doweling like a nailset to drive the dowel as you get close to the wood surface. Leave a little of the dowel extending past the surface on each side. Continue driving the second dowel into the hole, displacing the sharpened dowel, and use the driving dowel as the final peg.

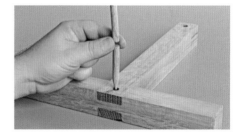

STEP 10: Unless you happened to find seat board stock that is more than 13" wide, you'll need to edge-glue at least two pieces to make the stock for the seat. Cut the pieces for the seat slightly oversize in length. To help with alignment, mark the mating edges of the parts for biscuits. Cut the biscuit slots with a biscuit joiner and then glue and clamp the top pieces together.

STEP 11: After the glue dries, remove the clamps and trim the top to finished size, Sand it thoroughly, working your way up to 220-grit.

STEP 12: The seat is attached by driving wood screws up through the top stretchers and into the underside of the seat. Drill counterbores and clearance holes in the top stretchers for attaching the seat. Do not use glue so the seat board can move slightly as humidity changes.

Drive the seat screws carefully, so they don't strip. Counterboring these holes allows you to decide precisely how far the screw will drive into the seat, instead of just relying on available screw lengths.

STEP 13: Apply a finish of your choice. I used polyurethane varnish.

"Zippered" Corner Shelf

This fun shelving project makes use of tricky corner space.

Everyone has at least a couple of free corners in their home. Here's a way to use that space. This curious shelf resembles the intriguing form of an automotive camshaft, and with a gravity-defying appearance to boot. Although it may look a little precarious, as if it is floating in the corner, once it's secured to the wall it is actually very solid. The shelf consists of thirteen parts: seven are the identical shelves, and they are separated by three pairs of progressively shorter vertical members.

Building this shelf will give you some valuable experience with dowel joinery (you can effectively use biscuit joints for this project if you prefer), as well as a clever way to set up a belt sander and use it as a stationary tool for precision sanding. You will enjoy the handy addition this shelf makes to your home storage roster: It manages to walk that fine line between being a focal point in the room and a quiet but practical design element.

"ZIPPERED" CORNER SHELF SHOPPING LIST

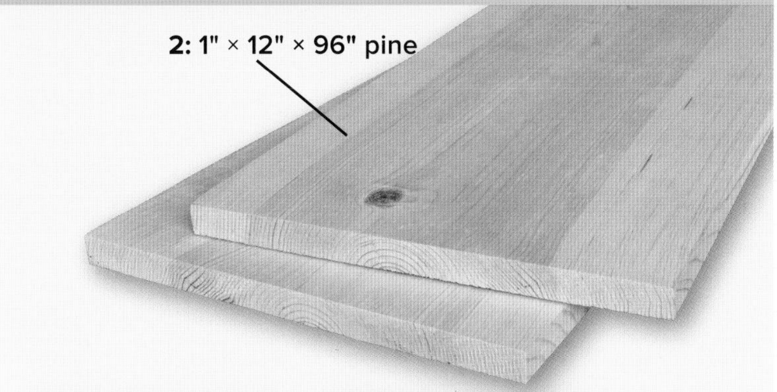

2: 1" × 12" × 96" pine

Wood glue

220-grit sanding belt with belt sander

Dark walnut stain

Polyurethane finish

▶ Sandpaper (120-, 220-grit)

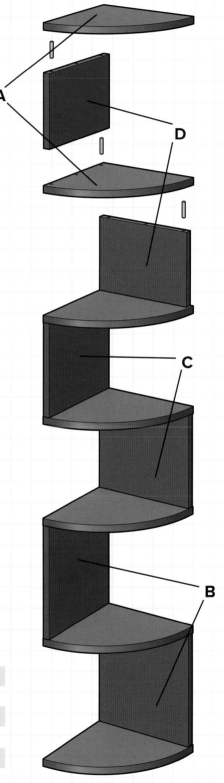

"ZIPPERED" CORNER SHELF CUT LIST

Overall Dimensions: 65¼" H × 11" D × 11" W

KEY	QTY	PART NAME	DIMENSION	MATERIAL
A	7	Shelf	¾" × 11" × 11"	Pine
B	2	Bottom Vertical	¾" × 11" × 12"	Pine
C	2	Center Vertical	¾" × 11" × 10"	Pine
D	2	Top Vertical	¾" × 11" × 8"	Pine

How to Build a "Zippered" Corner Shelf

STEP 1: Rip-cut ⅛" off each long edge of the 1 × 12 stock, using a circular saw and a straightedge cutting guide. This should reduce the "nominal" 1 × 12 to 11" in width. This is not a critical dimension as long as all of your 1 × 12 stock is reduced to uniform width.

STEP 2: Crosscut the vertical supports and shelf boards to length.

STEP 3: Lay out the arc for the rounded front edge on one of the shelves. I used an 11" radius for the profile, but this edge his doesn't have to be a perfect quarter circle; any eye-pleasing arc will do. You could even leave the front edges square.

STEP 4: Cut just outside the arc line on the first workpiece. A scrollsaw or bandsaw is ideal for this, but a jigsaw works fine as well.

STEP 5: Sand the arc smooth using the stationary belt sander technique shown on page 67—or, if you have a stationary sanding station use that. You can also use a sanding block for this step; it'll just take a lot longer.

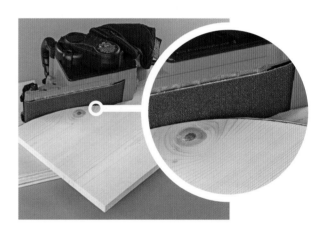

Sand just up to the profile line on the first shelf edge to get a smooth, fair curve. Use this shelf as a template for laying out the profiles on the other shelves.

STEP 6: Trace the arc onto the remaining shelves using the first shelf as a template. Cut and sand these as well.

STEP 7: Assemble the vertical members with the mating shelves to create two-and-three-part subassemblies. Drill guide holes for three dowels in the top and bottom edge of each vertical part (see Self-Centering Doweling Jig, page 69).

QUICK TIP

Creating Wider Stock

If your boards aren't wide enough to make the parts, you can edge-glue two narrower boards together. Assemble them using glue, dowels, or biscuits and clamps.

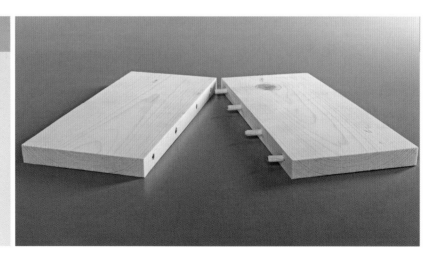

QUICK TIP

Stationary Belt Sander

Here's a trick you can use to make your belt sander function like a stationary sanding station. Lay your belt sander on its side on a flat piece of sheet stock and trace the outline of the tool edge onto the stock. Cut out this outline using a jigsaw. Screw the cutout piece to another piece of sheet stock of the same size. If necessary, use shims to make the belt surface perfectly perpendicular to the horizontal surface or base. This creates a recess where the tool body may rest out of the way and allow the bottom edge of the sanding belt to be below the surface of the jig so the surface may be used as a sanding table. Position the sander in the recess and then clamp the jig to your worksurface.

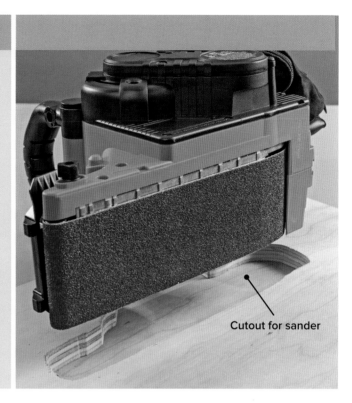

Cutout for sander

STEP 8: Press metal dowel centers into each dowel hole in the vertical supports and press the mating shelf parts against the vertical so the dowel centers leave a perfect drilling centerpoint on each shelf. Drill the guide holes into the shelves, using a depth stop to prevent drilling through the boards (see Quick Tip, pagfe 68).

STEP 9: Make the dowel joints to create the subassemblies using glue and clamps to draw the mating parts together.

STEP 10: Sand all the parts, working your way up to 220-grit. It's much easier to sand the parts prior to final assembly. After assembly, you can touch up any areas that need further attention, such as breaking over the visible sharp edges.

STEP 11: Join the subassemblies using glue, dowels, and clamps.

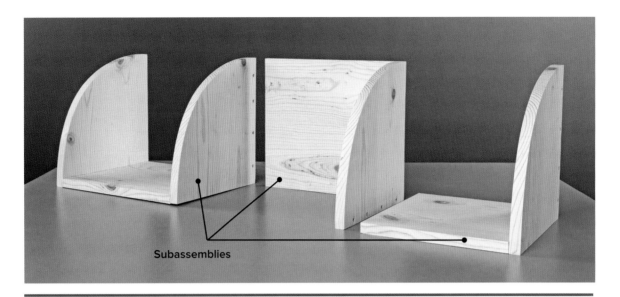

Subassemblies

Arrange the subassemblies together and assemble the shelf unit to completion using glue and dowels.

STEP 12: Apply a wood stain if you like. I chose a dark walnut stain for this piece.

STEP 13: Apply two or three coats of topcoat (I used polyurethane varnish). Allow the finish to dry then sand lightly with 400-grit paper between coats, wiping with a tack cloth before applying each coat.

STEP 14: Mount the shelf to the wall by screwing through the top two vertical supports into studs in a corner. Make sure to drill a clearance hole and countersink before attaching it to the wall. You can fill in the screw counterbore hole with wood putty if you wish and then color with the wood stain (or use tinted wood putty).

QUICK TIP

Depth Stop

Make a depth stop to make sure you don't drill through the workpiece. My favorite method is to cut a length of 1"-diameter dowel to the appropriate length and then drill a hole through the center. Seat the drilled dowel against your drill's chuck and you've got a foolproof way to bore holes of uniform depth. Perhaps the biggest benefit to dowel depth stops is that they do not degrade or shift as you use them, like masking tape or other popular stop materials can.

A 1" diameter dowel with a guide hole drilled through the center makes a foolproof drill stop.

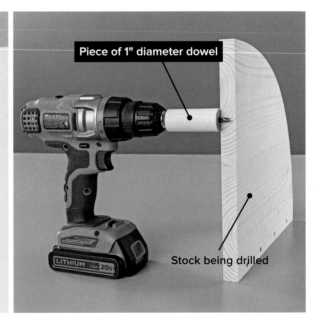

Piece of 1" diameter dowel

Stock being drilled

Self-Centering Doweling Jig

A self-centering doweling jig has one simple job and it does it well: to automatically register guide holes for dowel joints so the centerpoints fall precisely in the middle of a workpiece edge—thus allowing you to create joints with mating parts that are in perfect alignment. Also seen in this photo are dowel centers, which are fitted into guide holes to transfer the exact location of the dowel centerpoint on one workpiece onto the other when pressed against the mating part. This "Zippered" Corner Shelf is a perfect opportunity to use the doweling jig to center dowel holes on the edges of the verticals that mate with the flat shelves to make dowel joints. Then, use the dowel centers to transfer the exact locations of the holes in the board edges to the shelf surfaces.

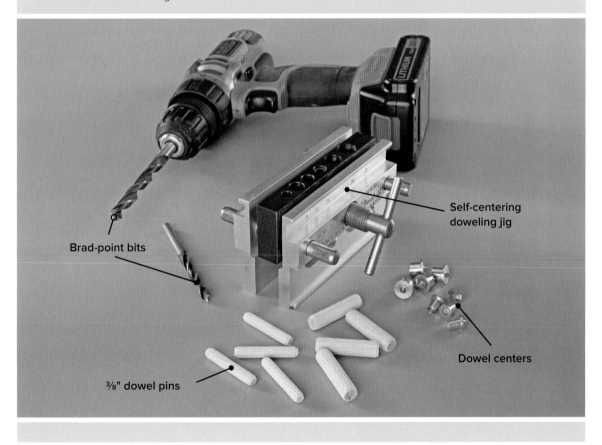

Brad-point bits

Self-centering doweling jig

Dowel centers

⅜" dowel pins

Kids' Chairs

Build these cute and sturdy kids chairs by the dozen (or just make one).

Whether it's out on the deck or at a kid-size work/play station, it's good to have safe, sturdy chairs sized for the little ones. Each of these chairs is fashioned from only six parts. If you plan to make a multitude of these chairs, use the router template provided here and take your time getting the template right. You can also create your own template design, altering the dimensions to suit different-sized kids. When the noisy and dusty stuff is done, bring the kids into the shop to help with assembly and painting. Make sure you use water-based paint, have everyone wear old clothes, and lay down a big sheet of plastic.

KIDS' CHAIRS SHOPPING LIST (2+ CHAIRS)

- ▶ ½" MDF for router template
- ▶ 1" wood screws
- ▶ Wood putty

- ▶ Sandpaper (120-, 180-, 220-grit)
- ▶ Paint primer
- ▶ Paint

Wood glue

1½" trim-head screws

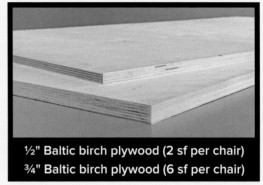

½" Baltic birch plywood (2 sf per chair)
¾" Baltic birch plywood (6 sf per chair)

QUICK TIP

Painting Wood

Finish-sand the wood. Remove all traces of sanding dust from the workpiece with a vaccuum or tack cloth.

Prime the wood with an even coat of primer (use water-based primer with water-based paint, and oil-based primer with oil-based paint). Smooth out brush marks as you work, and sand with 220-grit sandpaper when dry.

Apply a thin coat of paint, brushing with the grain. When dry, sand with 400-grit sandpaper, then wipe with a tack cloth. Apply at least one more heavier coat, sanding and wiping with a tack cloth between additional coats. Do not sand the last coat.

KIDS' CHAIRS CUT LIST (ONE CHAIR)

Overall Dimensions: 18" H × 11" D × 14" W

KEY	QTY	PART NAME	DIMENSION	MATERIAL
A	2	Leg	¾" × 14" × 18"	Baltic Birch
B	1	Front Stretcher	¾" x 2⁹⁄₁₆" × 8½"	Baltic Birch
C	1	Back Stretcher	¾" x 2" × 8½"	Baltic Birch
D	1	Seat	½" x 9" × 11"	Baltic Birch
E	1	Back	½" x 8" × 11"	Baltic Birch

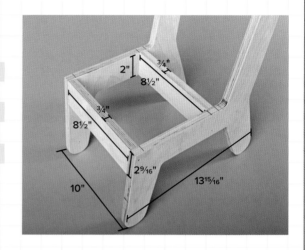

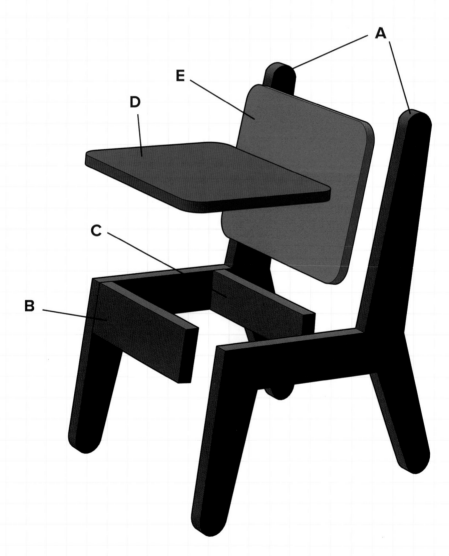

How to Build Kids' Chairs

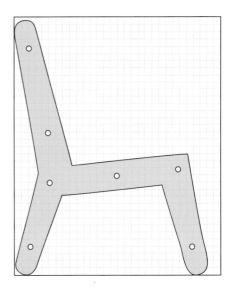

STEP 1: Transfer the scaled pattern to a piece of ½" MDF to make a router template for the chair legs: this is the trickiest part to make. Using ½"-thick stock for the template makes it easier to keep the bearing of the router bit on the template's edge.

STEP 2: Before cutting out the leg shape, drill ⅛" clearance holes for screws in the template, as shown in the diagram.

STEP 3: Trace the leg template onto the ¾" plywood stock. To be efficient, lay out all the legs at one time. Cut out the legs to rough shape using a jigsaw, staying slightly outside of the cutting lines. These parts (rough-cut but not finished) are called "blanks" by woodworkers.

FEATURED SKILL

Template Routing

Template routing is the best choice when you're making multiples of curved or odd-shaped parts. You'll need a router bit with a bearing at the top that's the same diameter as the bit's cutting flutes. It's called a pattern bit. The bearing rides against your template as the flutes cut your workpiece flush with the template. Take your time and make your template as perfect as possible. Any imperfections will show up on every piece you rout.

Trace your template onto your workpiece, and then cut out the piece, staying just outside the lines. If you use a jigsaw, install a fine-tooth wood-cutting blade so it doesn't tear out the plywood too badly. Fasten the template to the cutout

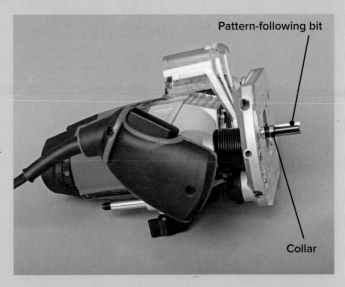

Pattern-following bit

Collar

workpiece using clamps, pin nails, or screws. If you're going to paint the project, screws are fine, as you'll fill the holes before painting anyway. If you're using screws, countersink them so that their heads are just below the template's surface so they don't impede the router's baseplate as you're sliding it along the template.

Clamp this assembly to a solid workbench and rout using the pattern bit. A router is a directional tool. For routing the outside of a shape, move the router counterclockwise. To rout an interior shape, such as the inside edge of a frame, move the router clockwise. Make sure to keep the router moving, so it doesn't cause burn spots on the workpiece.

When you lay out the legs, nest the
parts so you can get as many legs as
possible out of the same sheet.

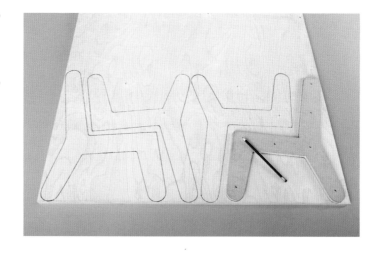

STEP 4: The chair legs are tooled to final
shape and size with a router and pattern-
following straight bit. These bits have a
bearing at the top or bottom that follows
the edge of the template to position the
straight cutting bit. Tack the template to
one of the leg blanks with screws, driven
through the pilot holes in the template.
Center the template within the profile you
cut. Clamp the assembly to your bench,
and rout the leg edges flush with the pattern (see below). You'll need to move the clamps and rotate the assembly
a few times to get router access so you can rout all the edges. Repeat on the rest of the leg blanks.

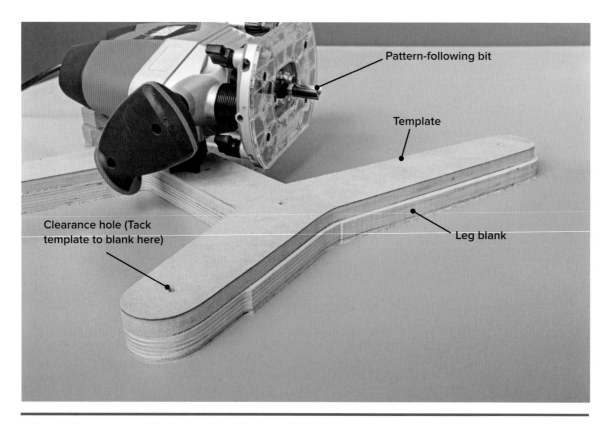

Pattern-following bit

Template

Clearance hole (Tack
template to blank here)

Leg blank

Attach the router template to each leg blank, tacking with screws driven through the clearance holes in
the template. Use a router and pattern-following bit to trim the blanks to final size.

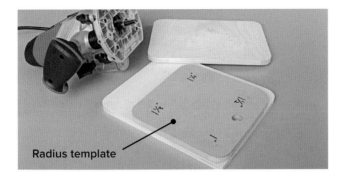

Radius template

Here's a great shop aid if you want to build your skills with a router. Make a radius template with common roundover radius sizes tooled into each corner (here, from 1" to 1½"). Use the template as a pattern with a pattern bit to make smooth, uniform radius cuts. Here, the template is being positioned to make a 1"-radius on a seat.

STEP 5: Cut the stretchers from ¾"-thick stock, using a table saw or circular saw and straightedge cutting guide. Also cut the seats and backs from ½"-thick stock. Radius the corners of the seat and back, so there are no sharp corners.

STEP 6: Mark the stretcher locations on the legs, using your template as a guide, and then drill clearance holes for screws.

STEP 7: Attach the legs to the stretchers with wood screws and glue.

Clamp the stretchers and legs together to test the fit and make any necessary adjustments. Then, remove the clamps, glue the joints, reclamp the joints, and drive the wood screws to reinforce them.

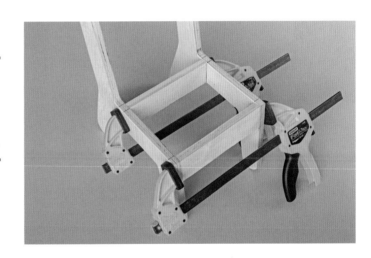

STEP 8: Attach the seat and back using glue and trim-head screws. Fill the screw head holes with wood putty or joint compound and sand the whole chair, working your way up to 220-grit. Round over the sharp edges.

STEP 9: Apply primer, let it dry, and paint the chair. If you want to paint the frame a different color than the seats and backs, use painter's tape to ensure clean lines.

QUICK TIP

Gluing before Painting

I don't paint the parts before assembly because I want a strong glue joint. Wood glue will stick to water-based paint, but it's not as strong as gluing bare wood to bare wood. You could mask off the gluing surfaces prior to painting. If you're using a water-based dye, you can apply that first, as it's not a surface coating.

Open Display Shelf

Vertical lines meet horizontal lines and the result is a display shelf with deep roots in high design.

Designing your own carpentry and woodworking projects is a fun and gratifying exercise, but the more you design, the more you will realize that there is not actually much new under the sun. Most of what we do is customizing and refining objects and furniture that have come before us. This tall display shelf is a splendid example of a form that was created a long time ago and simply requires a little updating to become the project you see here.

Here is where this project has its roots. Starting in the Netherlands in 1917, the De Stijl (Dutch for "The Style") design movement focused on using basic geometric shapes. In furniture, this translated into breaking things down to their basic elements: horizontal and vertical lines. One of the most iconic pieces from the De Stijl movement is the Red and Blue Chair (see page 153) by Gerrit Rietveld.

For my interpretation of this shelf, I returned to the same well for inspiration. Its construction is straightforward and elementary, but by applying some De Stijl-ery, an ordinary shelf becomes something visually appealing made with modern materials available at most building centers. You could use the same color scheme as the chair on page 146; I decided to leave this one natural.

OPEN DISPLAY SHELF SHOPPING LIST

Wood glue

Trim-head screws

Wood finish

▶ Sandpaper (120-, 180-, 220-grit)
▶ Wood putty

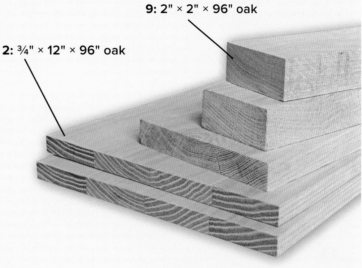

9: 2" × 2" × 96" oak

2: ¾" × 12" × 96" oak

FEATURED TOOL

Zero-Clearance Miter Saw Table

Glue a plywood fence to a ¼"-thick base, and attach it to your miter saw using screws driven through the saw's fence. This attachment serves two purposes: It eliminates tear-out on the back side of your parts, and the kerf in the fence gives you an exact location to line up your cutting marks.

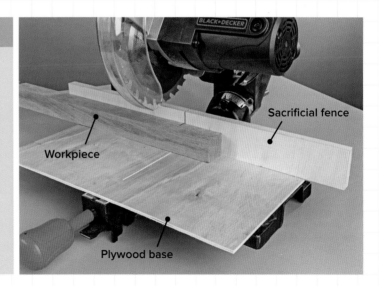

Workpiece

Sacrificial fence

Plywood base

OPEN DISPLAY SHELF CUT LIST

Overall Dimensions: 60" H × 16¾" D × 23" W

KEY	QTY	PART NAME	DIMENSION	MATERIAL
A	4	Post	1½" × 1½" × 60"	Oak
B	10	Front Rung	1" × 1" × 23"	Oak
C	10	Side Rung	1" × 1" × 16¾"	Oak
D	5	Shelf	¾" × 11¼" × 23"	Oak

1"
Front
overhang

1½"
Side
overhang

How to Build an Open Display Shelf

STEP 1: Cut the legs and rungs to finished length and then sand them smooth. Break the sharp corners using a sanding block or block plane.

Don't be afraid of hand planes. Most beginners who have tried using a block plane or any of the more common hand plane types have ended up with workpieces that are gouged and disappointing. But keep trying—a well-honed plane is an indispensable tool for experienced woodworkers. Getting good results is just a matter of patience and practice (and keeping the blades sharp). For this project, a block plane made quick work of adding a tiny chamfer to all the edges, which is more atttractive then the rounding you get with a sanding block.

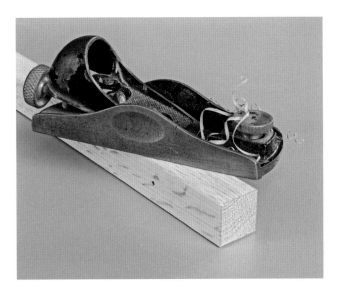

STEP 2: Make pairs of spacer blocks for accurately positioning the rungs on the front and back pairs of legs. It may seem like overkill, but alignment is a critical aspect of the success of this project and there is no more foolproof method than with spacer blocks.

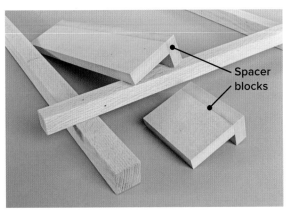

Spacer blocks

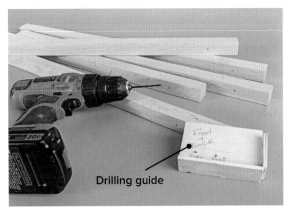

Drilling guide

Spacer blocks made to the exact length of the distances between shelves ensure that the alignment will be perfect. These are made from scraps of MDF that were pin-nailed together with a pneumatic nailer.

Make a drilling guide to predrill all the rungs, ensuring consistency of position to avoid errors. This guide was made with ⅜ and ¼" plywood scraps.

STEP 3: Attach the rungs all the way up the pairs of front and back legs using glue and trim-head screws. Check the assembly for square as you go, making any necessary adjustments before the glue dries.

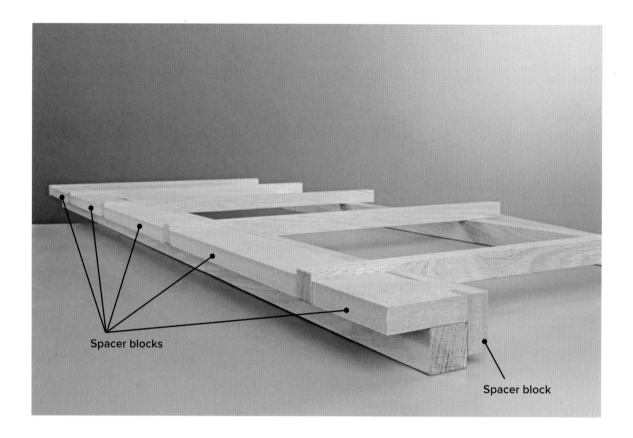

Spacer blocks

Spacer block

Lay the legs on a flat surface and position the spacer blocks on top of them, then attach the rungs at the predrilled locations with glue and trim-head screws.

STEP 4: Clamp two side rungs—one at the top and one at the bottom—between the front and back ladders using the block you made to register the overhang to get the distance right.

STEP 5: Glue all the mating surfaces and attach the middle side rungs using trim-head screws. Remove the clamps and attach the top and bottom rungs as well. Fasten the other set of side rungs.

STEP 6: Cut the shelves to fit and then sand them, breaking all the sharp corners with a sanding block or block plane.

STEP 7: Fill the screw holes with wood putty if desired and then sand smooth. Apply a finish to the stand and the shelves before installing the shelves. (I did not stain this but chose to use only a clear, protective topcoat of varnish.)

STEP 8: Screw the shelves to the rungs using 1½" trim-head screws driven from the underside of the rungs.

Gluing and Clamping

Assembling a project is a bit like dancing—a matter of coordination and timing. All the parts, equipment, and supplies must be in the right place, and you need to know where they are so you can work quickly and complete the assembly before the glue sets. If a project is simple and has few parts, it can usually be assembled in one session. But complex projects may need to be assembled in stages or as subassemblies.

Determining the sequence of gluing parts should be done with a dry run. here's a quick overview of a typical assembly:

- Have some cardboard or pads handy to protect the projecting from marring.

- Check to make sure that all of the project's parts fit together correctly by assembling them without glue.

- Determine how many and what types of clamps are needed. Adjust the clamp jaws close to the required opening distance so they can be quickly tightened and then stage them in convenient spots around the assembly area.

- Gather all the other supplies that might be needed, including glue, a glue brush or spreader, rags, dowels or biscuits, a tape measure (to check for square), masking tape, a scraper or putty knife, clamp pads, a rubber mallet, and a few blocks of soft wood.

- Start applying glue to the joints. Spread the glue evenly—not too wet and not too dry—and on all mating surfaces (if using yellow glue). Work quickly so the glue doesn't have a chance to set.

- Begin clamping by placing all the clamps with light pressure, and then tighten them sequentially but don't overtighten.

- In the case of a cabinet, check for square by measuring diagnally across the corners with a tape measure. Adjust if necessary.

- Glue squeeze-out is almost inevitable, but you can keep it from staining around joints by carefully applying masking tape to the adjoining edges of the joints before clamping. If that's not practical, wipe away the excess glue with a damp cloth or wait until it sets to a rubbery consistency and remove it with a sharp chisel.

- Leave the clamps on until the glue cures, which can be as long as 24 hours for yellow glue.

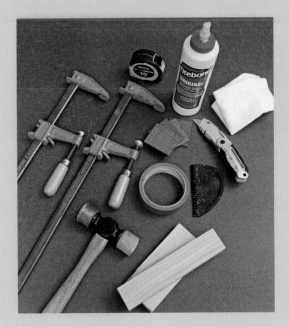

The best way to avoid panic when assembling a project is to stage all the items you typically use so you don't need to go looking for them.

Hickory Knickknack Shelves

Elegant lines, a simple design, and beautiful wood tones give these shelves a nautical feel.

The joinery used to make these knickknack shelves may look a little intimidating at first, but it really is done with just a few notches and some dadoes. The joints make for a rugged connection between the shelves and the uprights. Also, the uprights are spaced at 16" on center—standard wall stud spacing—so the keyhole hangers used here allow an invisible yet very sturdy connection to the wall (if you decide to hang the shelf unit so it aligns with the wall studs). Gentle curves on the front edges of the shelves draw the eye and beg to be touched. The shelves are strong enough to hold large, heavy books, but you may want to store something smaller on them so you can still admire the beautiful hickory tones and your fine wood joinery.

HICKORY KNICKKNACK SHELVES SHOPPING LIST

*HICKORY is a hard, durable wood that is used primarily for flooring and cabinetry these days (there was a time when one of its major uses was for baseball bats). Because of its relative hardness, it can be tough to work with if you are using hand tools. Most lumberyards stock it in predimensioned sizes as well as in random widths and lengths. You can usually find it in dimensional, S4S (sanded four sides) stock at larger building centers as well, but it is often a special-order item, so allow some time for it to arrive. It does not take wood stains especially well, but with its distinctive brown and white figure, it looks lovely with just a clear topcoat.

▶ Sandpaper (120-, 180-grit)

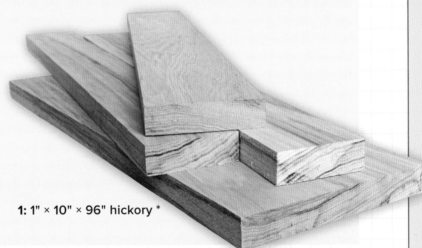

1: 1" × 10" × 96" hickory *

Wood glue

Keyhole hangers

FEATURED HARDWARE

Keyhole Hangers

Keyhole hangers are recessed into the back of a shelf to provide hooks on which to hang the shelf. When you're using two hangers (such as on this shelving unit), take care to locate them in the exact same position on both pieces. Trace the hanger in its position. Keyhole hangers are usually rounded on their ends. If you have a small router or rotary tool, you can use it to cut the recess as well as the curve. If you don't have either of those tools, use a chisel and make the ends square.

Continue this process until you reach the correct depth for your hangers. Screw the hangers in their recesses. Usually the screws that come with the hangers are quite short—I used 1½"-long screws of the same diameter and head size just to make sure the hangers were secure.

Start by tapping the chisel in around the outline of the recess. Pare away a layer of the recess and then tap around the edges again.

KNICKKNACK SHELF CUT LIST

Overall Dimensions: 23" H × 8" D × 24½" W

KEY	QTY	PART NAME	DIMENSION	MATERIAL
A	1	Top Shelf	¾" × 4" × 24½"	Hickory
B	1	Middle Shelf	¾" × 6" × 24½"	Hickory
C	1	Bottom Shelf	¾" × 8" × 24½"	Hickory
D	2	Support	¾" × 3" × 26"	Hickory

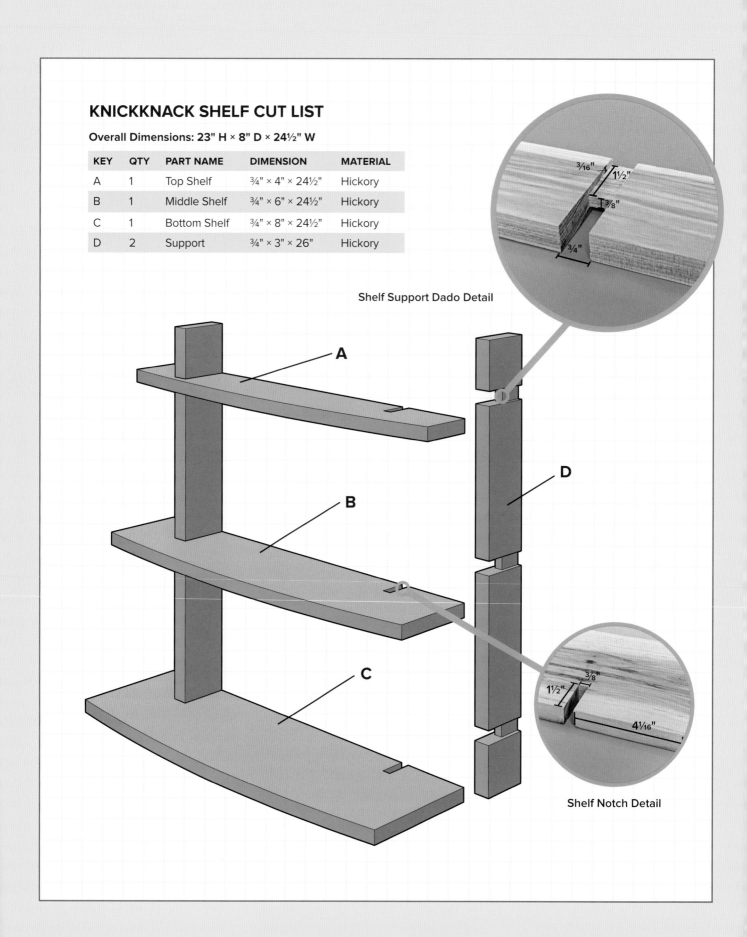

Shelf Support Dado Detail

Shelf Notch Detail

How to Build Hickory Knickknack Shelves

STEP 1: These knickknack shelves can be fashioned from a single 8' piece of 1 × 10 hickory (or another species of your choosing) if you lay out your parts carefully. If you are building from random-width stock, you will need to dress the lumber before you start cutting. This is normally done using a planer, jointer, and table saw, but if the stock you have is already planed to consistent thickness (¾" as shown), you can cut it into usable strips with a circular saw (install a rip-cutting blade) and a straightedge cutting guide (see page 127). After dimensioning and laying out your parts, cut the shelves to finished size, but let them remain rectangular for now—you'll curve the front edges later.

STEP 2: Cut the ⅜"-wide by 1½" deep notches in the shelves. A table saw fitted with a dado blade set is the best way to make the notches, using a double miter gauge and a stop block (see page 97). Make multiple passes using a single blade. Rotate the shelves 180° to cut the notch at the other end.

If you have a stacked dado set, use it to cut the notches, making several passes and raising the blade after all the shelves have been cut at each pass. You'll need to install a zero-clearance throat plate (see page 26) and a sacrificial miter gauge fence when using the dado blade set.

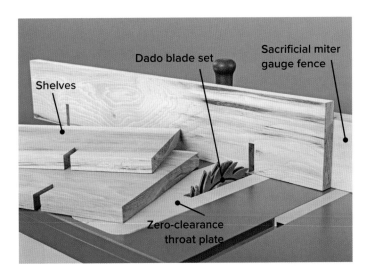

STEP 3: Sand the shelves after cutting their notches. Sand lightly around the notches so you don't significantly change the shelves' thickness.

QUICK TIP

Before finish-sanding the shelves, draw some light pencil lines on the surfaces of the boards. Sand with progressively finer grits until the pencil marks have been erased. This will help you to maintain even board thickness by avoiding oversanding in some areas.

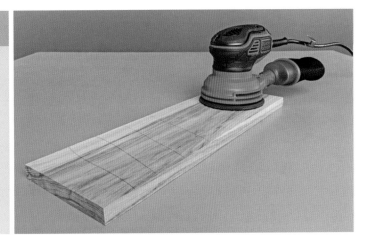

STEP 4: Cut the uprights to final dimension. Each upright is milled with aligned dado grooves on both faces. The dado grooves are then notched to fit over the shelves when the upright slides into the shelf notches. Use the same basic setup to cut these joints as you did for the notches. I used a double-miter gauge and stopblock set up.

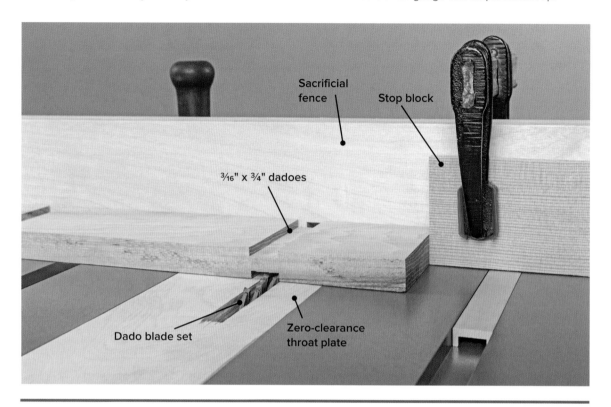

After cutting the first set of dadoes on each face of both uprights, reset the stop block to cut each of the remaining sets of dadoes.

Use a handsaw and sharp chisel to notch out the uprights between the dado grooves. A Japanese handsaw called a *dozuki* is shown here: these saws are popular with woodworkers for their ease of control when doing precise work because they cut on the more manageable pull stroke. Sand the uprights, working your way up to 180-grit.

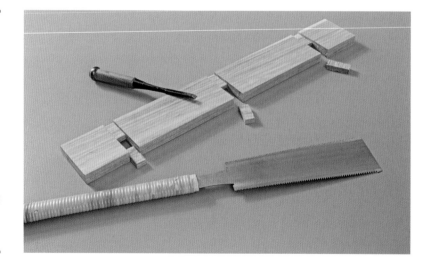

STEP 5: The easiest way to remove the wood between the aligned dado grooves in the uprights is to cut the shoulders of the notches with a handsaw and then clean up the bottoms of the notches with a sharp wood chisel.

STEP 6: Lay out the curve on the front edge of the shelves using the slat-and-string layout method shown on page 101. Cut the curve with a jigsaw or bandsaw. Sand to the line using a stationary belt sander (page 67). Ease the sharp edges with a sanding block or block plane.

STEP 7: Apply glue to the notches and slide the shelves into position. Drill pilot holes and countersinks and attach the shelves from the back using screws.

The shelves fit into the notched dadoes in the uprights. The mechanical connection is strong enough to support the shelves, but glue and screw them from the backs of the uprights to hold them in place.

STEP 8: Lay out the recesses for the keyhole hangers in the backs of each upright. Cut these recesses using a chisel or a router. If you choose to rout them, use a ⅛"-diameter bit. The depth is shallow enough that it's easy to rout these freehand. Apply a finish of your choice— I used clear wood varnish only.

"Celebrating Plywood" Coffee Table

A cute table that elevates ordinary plywood to eye-grabbing heights.

This elegant little table celebrates simple materials: exterior plywood and MDF. What makes the table come to life is the orientation of the plywood and the fascinating patterns and textures created when the plywood laminations are exposed. Anyone who's cut plywood has certainly noticed the unexpected attractiveness of the layered laminations on a cut edge. Why not feature it? By cutting strips of plywood and turning them on edge, butcher-block style, you end up with a surface that resembles bamboo and has a very on-trend industrial sensibility. The crisscrossing base is a chance to practice some basic joinery, employing bridle joints as well as a half-lap.

"CELEBRATING PLYWOOD" COFFEE TABLE SHOPPING LIST

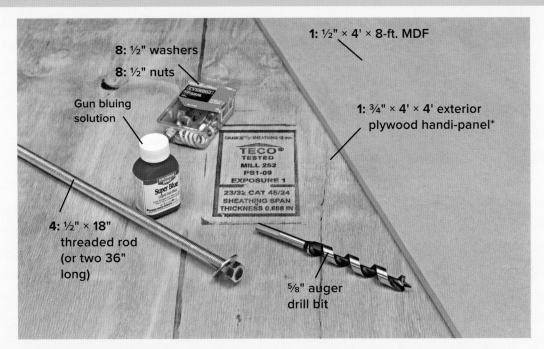

The tabletop is made from strips of exterior plywood laminated together. The base is from a triple layer of ½" MDF. Threaded rod (also called by the brand name All-Thread) is used to pin the plywood strips together. A ⅝"-diameter auger drill bit makes clean guide holes for the threaded rod. Gun bluing is a solution that creates a chemical reaction in metal to darken it and prevent rust.

*HANDI-PANELS are cut-down sizes of common sheet goods sold at most building centers. You can usually find them in the most common types and thicknesses, with sizes including 2 × 4', 2 × 8', and 4 × 4', depending on the store. You'll pay a bit more per square foot, but buying them reduces waste and makes the sheet goods easily transportable. If you can't find precut handi-panels, many building centers and lumberyards will cut them down for you—sometimes even free of charge, as long as you purchase the full sheet.

4: 1½ × 1½" L-brackets with screws
- Sanding belts (60-, 120-grit)
- Sanding disc (180-grit)
- Paint

- Clear topcoat
- Joint compound or wood putty
- Wood glue

"CELEBRATING PLYWOOD" CUT LIST

Approximate Overall Dimensions: 13" H × 18¼" D × 39⅝" W

KEY	QTY	PART NAME	DIMENSION	MATERIAL
A	24	Top Strips	¾" x 1¾" x 40"	Exterior Plywood
B	8	Outer Base Uprights	½" x 3" x 11"	MDF
C	4	Inner Base Uprights	½" x 3" x 8"	MDF
D	1	Inner Short Section	½" x 3" x 14"	MDF
E	2	Outer Short Section	½" x 3" x 8"	MDF
F	1	Inner Long Section	½" x 3" x 32"	MDF
G	2	Outer Long Section	½" x 3" x 26"	MDF

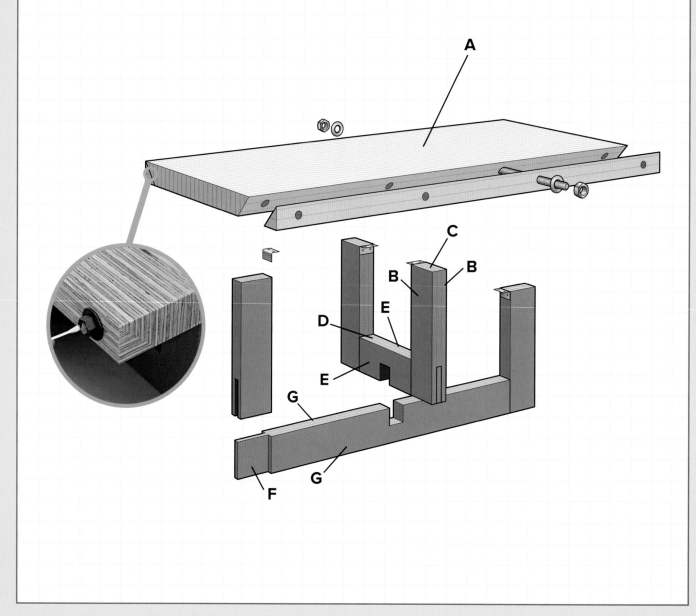

How to Build a "Celebrating Plywood" Coffee Table

STEP 1: Start by cutting the plywood strips that are used to create the laminated plywood tabletop. I used ¾" exterior plywood sheathing (actual thickness is ²³⁄₃₂"). If you have access to a table saw, it will make quick work of this step. Otherwise, use a circular saw and a straightedge. Cut the strips all from the same piece, cutting in the same direction, generally with the grain of the plywood surfaces. Clean up the strips to remove any splinters or tear-out.

STEP 2: Dry-assemble the strips for the whole tabletop, moving and shifting individual strips until you find the arrangement you desire. Exterior plywood has voids, so try to choose the nicest-looking edges for the tops of the strips.

Dry-lay the plywood strips for the tabletop so the cleanest edges are facing upward. Number the strips with a pencil to set their order, indicating which edges face upward.

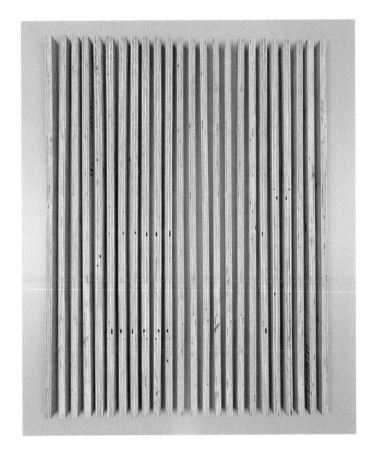

STEP 3: Select the two sets of three strips from the outer edges, apply wood glue to the mating faces, and clamp them together until the glue has dried, with the edges and ends flush.

STEP 4: The two outer strip assemblies are bevel-cut along the long edges to continue the top texture along the edges and create a more decorative corner. This is not as hard to do as it sounds. If you have a table saw, just set up the saw for a 45° bevel cut and rip the outside edges. If you are using a circular saw and straightedge, set the blade to cut at 45° and secure the workpiece. To provide some extra bearing surface for the saw foot, place the other set of strips next to the one being cut. Make the 45° bevels cuts along the edge of one workpiece so the saw kerf hits at the corner of the workpiece. Trade the workpieces and then bevel-cut the other edge. Then, simply rotate the offcuts and glue them back onto the workpieces, oriented so that the plywood edge now shows as the edge of the table. Glue and tack the new edges in place using finish nails (a pneumatic pin nailer is perfect for this if you have air tools).

STEP 5: Gang two or three plywood strips together and clamp them to your worksurface, placing some scrap wood beneath the bottom strip to help prevent tearout from the drill. Lay out drilling points and drill guide holes for the threaded rods on the top strip and carefully bore the guide holes at the drilling points. Make a drilling guide (see page 92) by fastening two wood scraps at a right angle (or use a drill press if you have access to one). Use this assembly to keep the drill bit vertical if you are using a hand-held drill.

Use two pieces of square scrap wood joined at a right angle as a drilling guide to keep the bit aligned as you drill the guide holes for the threaded rod into the plywood laminate strips.

STEP 6: Drill all the strips using the first strips you drilled as a spacing guide for the drilling centerpoints. Also drill guide holes in the outer assemblies. With the new edges on a sacrificial board, drill the holes all the way through these sections.

Finish drilling the guide holes for the threaded rods, including the two outer sections.

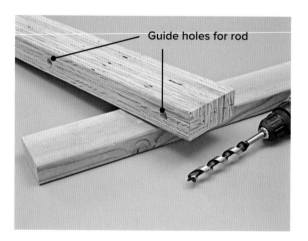

Guide holes for rod

STEP 7: Arrange the laminate strips and sections on a flat surface. Slide a threaded rod with a nut and washer through each hole in one of the outer edge sections and guide it through the aligned holes. Install all threaded rods, keeping some clearance between strips. Apply glue to the mating faces and then clamp the strips together with pipe or bar clamps. To help maintain a flat top, glue on the strips in stages, three or four at a time. When you're done, thread nuts and washers onto the ends of the threaded rods.

Clamp the tabletop with pipe or bar clamps until the glue dries. Once you have removed the clamps, it will likely take some heavy sanding with a belt sander to get a smooth, even surface on the tabletop.

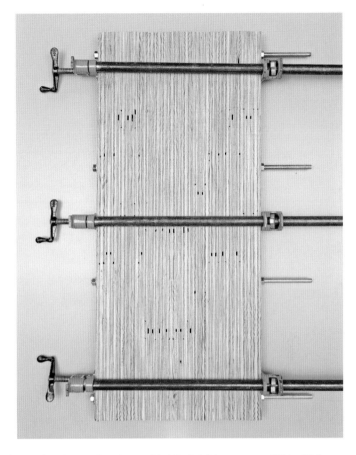

STEP 8: Once the glue dries, trim the ends of the tabletop flush and square using a circular saw with a guide (as shown on page 127).

STEP 9: To flatten and smooth the top surface of the tabletop, use a belt sander. Start with a 60-grit belt, and work your way up to 120-grit. Clean off the sawdust and fill any voids with wood putty. Finish the sanding with 180-grit on a random orbit sander. Also sand the edges and underside of the tabletop lightly. Apply a finish of your choice—I used three thin coats of polyurethane varnish. Set the tabletop aside.

STEP 10: The table base is made with two three-part assemblies that fit together in a half-lap joint. Each assembly is made with three pieces of ½"-thick MDF that are fastened together to create a type of bridle joint (see pages 58 to 63 for more on making bridle joints). Since all the base parts are 3" wide, start by ripping your MDF stock into 3"-wide strips and cut them to length according to the cutting list.

The individual members of the leg base are each made from three strips of ½" MDF, joined together to create mortises and tenons.

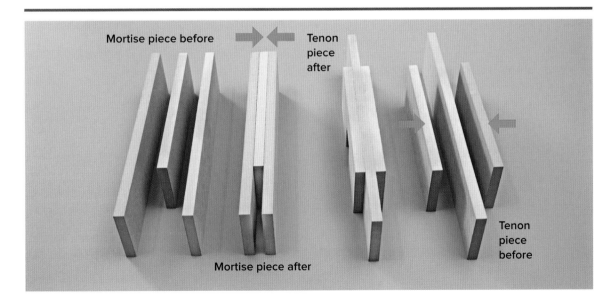

Mortise piece before

Tenon piece after

Mortise piece after

Tenon piece before

STEP 11: Glue the three parts for each of the two base assemblies, creating mortises and tenons. Let the glue dry.

STEP 12: In the middle, horizontal member of each assembly, cut a 1½ × 1½" notch to make the half-lap joints. There are many ways you can do this, including a table saw with a dado blade set (see page 51) or a jig saw.

STEP 13: Assemble the three-part leg assemblies, gluing the bridle joints.

Glue the two three-part leg assemblies together, and be sure to orient the notches so they will overlap and form a half-lap joint.

1½" × 1½" notch

Bridle joint "tenon"

Bridle joint "mortise"

STEP 14: Fill any gaps in the base with spackle or wood putty and then sand them. Ease the sharp corners with a sanding block.

STEP 15: Join the base components, applying glue to the half-lap joint.

Glue the half-lap joint together to form the two base parts into the table base. Paint the base.

STEP 16: Flip the tabletop upside down on a protected worksurface. Center the base and then attach the base to the tabletop with 1½ × 1½" L-brackets. Make sure you predrill the screw holes.

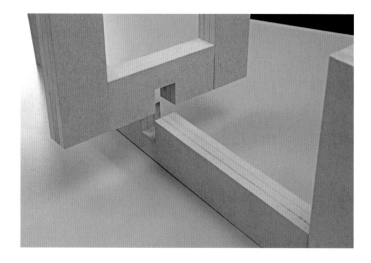

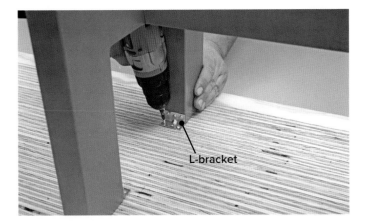

L-bracket

Attach the base to the tabletop with L-brackets and screws.

STEP 17: To give the nuts and washers an aged look, use a bluing solution to darken them before reinstalling.

STEP 18: Cut the ends of the threaded rod flush with the nuts, clean off any metal burrs with emery paper, and then use a cotton swab or rag to apply bluing solution the ends of the threaded rod.

Apply bluing solution to the cut ends of the threaded rods so they match the washers and nuts.

QUICK TIP

Using Gun-bluing Solution

Gun-bluing solution is a thin liquid that is applied to metal to darken it and help protect it from rusting. It is called "bluing solution" because it is used to treat the steel barrels of guns—the chemical, when applied to raw steel, creates an instant reaction with the metal that gives it a deep, black, permanent tint.

Before   During   After

Exotic Shelf

Any interesting hardwood will be front-and-center in this trim shelf unit.

Here's another take on a small display shelf. It's similar in construction to the shelf on page 82, but simpler, as there is only one back support. Like the other shelf, the joinery is very strong, and you'll attach it directly to a wall stud so it'll hold whatever you can fit on it. Because of its small size, this is a fantastic opportunity to visit your local lumberyard and find some really impressive wood. I hadn't had the opportunity to make anything using padauk (pronounced *pa-dook)* before, so I decided to give that a go. But any of the more common hardwood will work—you can even finish them with mahogany stain for a purplish cast that is not unlike the padauk.

EXOTIC SHELF SHOPPING LIST

Hardwood (padauk* is shown here):
• You can make this entire project from a single 1 x 8 x 96" hardwood board, with some nice cutoff pieces left over. But since most exotic hardwood is rather expensive, you can shop for the following "standard" board sizes (nominal) to economize on materials:

▶ **1: 1" × 8" × 24" (D)**
▶ **1: 1" × 6" × 60" (A, B, C, E)**

*PADAUK is an African wood prized for its striking red-orange color. It's readily available at most lumberyards and is comparable in price to black walnut. Despite its weight and density, padauk can be worked relatively easily with power tools. Wear a dust mask or respirator when working with padauk, as some people are sensitive to the dust and oils produced from cutting and sanding.

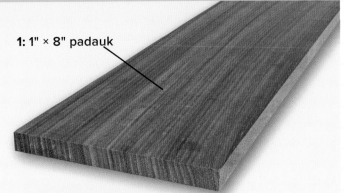

1: 1" × 8" padauk

▶ **Sanding belt (180-grit)**
▶ **Sandpaper (120-, 180-grit)**
▶ **Wood glue**
▶ **Paste wax**
▶ **1½" wood screws**

FEATURED TOOLS
Double Miter Gauge

If you will be cutting or tooling small parts on your table saw, invest in a second miter gauge (the pushing tool that fits into the slots in the saw table). A second miter gauge increases the control you have over the parts. Slide each gauge into a miter slot on each side of the blade on the saw table. Create a custom fence for the setup by face-gluing two ¾" × 3½" × 30" pieces of MDF or plywood. Fasten the fence to both miter gauges using screws driven through the holes in the miter gauges. Secure your workpiece to the fence and feed the setup through the saw using both hands. Having a second gauge reduces vibration and movement as the workpiece passes over the blade.

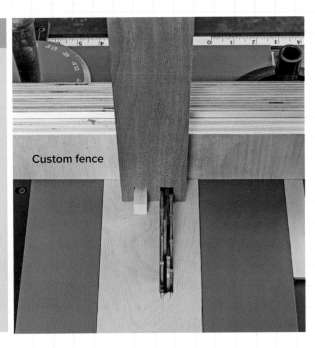

Custom fence

EXOTIC SHELF CUT LIST

Overall Dimensions: 32" H × 6½" D × 18" W

KEY	QTY	PART NAME	DIMENSION	MATERIAL
A	1	Shelf 1	¾" × 4" × 12"	Padauk
B	1	Shelf 2	¾" × 5" × 14"	Padauk
C	1	Shelf 3	¾" × 5½" × 16"	Padauk
D	1	Shelf 4	¾" × 6½" × 18"	Padauk
E	1	Support	¾" × 4" × 32"	Padauk

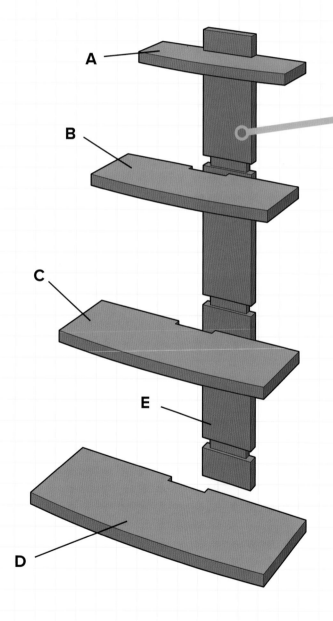

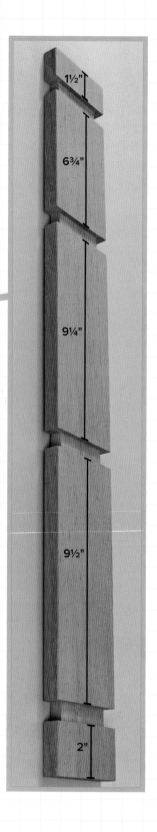

How to Build an Exotic Shelf

STEP 1: Cut the shelves and back support to length and width. Feel free to adjust the sizes a little bit according to what you can reap from your stock. If you have nominal 1 × 4 stock, for example, you can make the support and the top shelf 3½" wide (actual width of 1 × 4) instead of 4" wide—just remember to make proportional adjustments to the other parts, too.

STEP 2: Lay out the curves on the front edges of the shelves. The slat-and-string method detailed on page 101 will work well for this. All four shelves should have the same radius curve.

STEP 3: Cut the curves with a jigsaw or bandsaw. Sand the curves so they are smooth and even, using a sanding station or a belt sander on edge.

The back support is milled with a notched dado at each shelf location.

STEP 4: Cut the ¾"-wide by ¼"-deep dadoes at each shelf location in the back support. This works best using a dado set in a tablesaw. If you don't have a dado set, you can make multiple passes using a single blade or hand-cut the dadoes with a saw or just a wood chisel.

STEP 5: Make ½"-deep shoulder cuts at the end of each dado in the back support.

You can cut the shoulders using a table saw with a dado blade set or just a single blade. You can also use a handsaw and chisel out the waste.

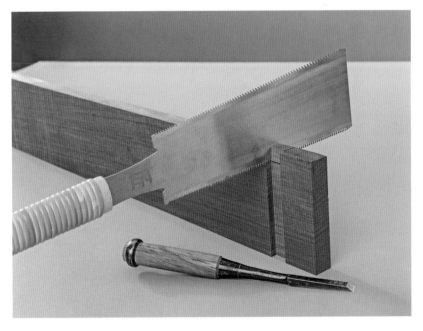

STEP 6: Lay out the ½"-deep by 3"-wide notches at the back of each shelf and cut them using a tablesaw with a dado set and double miter gauge (page 97) or cut them by hand with a saw and chisel

A ½"-deep notch is cut into the back of each shelf to make a dado joint with the back support.

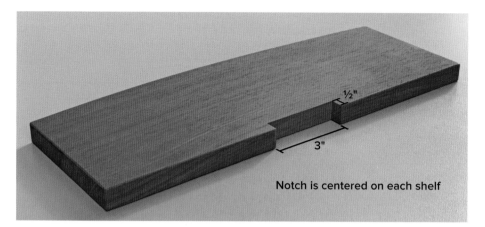

½"

3"

Notch is centered on each shelf

QUICK TIP

Paste wax is not the most common wood finish, but it is one of the simplest and it has the unique advantage of being easily refreshed. In the container, the wax molecules are suspended in a solvent that helps them penetrate into the wood pores when the paste wax is applied. Once the wax dries (once the solvent evaporates), the wax remains behind and can be buffed to a high gloss without being wiped from the wood. The more you buff, the shinier the finish becomes. A shelf such as this is not likely to undergo wear and tear, so you will probably never need to strip and reapply the wax. But if you use paste wax on a furnishing that is subject to scratching and other damage, you can restore the finish by stripping off the wax using a rag dampened with the original solvent. Then, you simply repeat the paste wax application for a finish that is brand-new. The only significant drawback to using paste wax (presuming you don't mind doing some hand buffing) is that it does not resist spillage of wine or any other liquid containing alcohol.

To apply paste wax, rub it on using a rag or 0000 (extrafine) steel wool. When it's dry (in about 5 minutes), buff the wax using a cotton rag or, for larger surfaces, an electric polisher with a soft, absorbent bonnet.

Laying Out Curves with a Slat and String

There are many ways to lay out a smooth curve or arc. One of the easiest and most reliable—especially for shallower curves such as the shelf fronts on this project—is to fashion a springy wood slat and a length of cotton string (cotton string will not stretch like many synthetics will). To lay out a curve, cut a strip of wood that's ⅛" thick, 1" wide, and whatever length you need. For these shelves, a 36"-long strip is sufficient. Drill a small hole at one end, centered top to bottom. Cut a slot about 1" long in the other end of the strip, also centered top to bottom and perpendicular to the end. Use a handsaw or jigsaw to cut the slot. Pass a piece of string through the hole, and then tie a knot large enough to not pull back through the hole. Cut the string off about a foot longer than the strip of wood. Bend the strip to the approximate arc radius you want, then pull the string end through the slot, securing it. Tighten or loosen the string until you have achieved the exact curve you are after, then wrap the string around the slotted end of the strip a couple of times to keep the string from moving in the slot. Set the slat and string onto the workpiece so the centerlines of the strip and the workpiece align. Trace the curved wood strip onto the workpiece to create your curved cutting line.

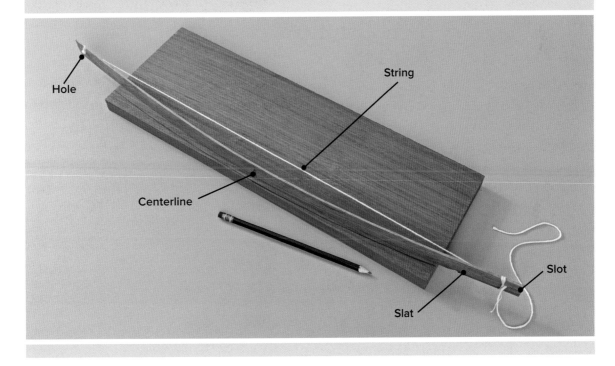

STEP 7: Sand all the parts. Be careful not to sand too aggressively around the notches as you don't want to significantly change the thickness.

STEP 8: Predrill two screw holes through each dado in the back support. Countersink these holes from the back side.

STEP 9: Dry-fit each shelf and drill pilot holes into the shelves for the screws.

STEP 10: Install the shelves using glue. Screw the shelves in place from the back. Finish as desired. I used paste wax for a warm sheen and to deepen the natural red tone of the padauk.

Oak Step Stool

An eminently useful step stool teaches valuable lessons in joinery.

My mother says that at one point in her life, she reached the towering height of 5'1". I'm not sure I believe her. Our kitchen countertops were 4" lower than a standard kitchen counter, so she could use them comfortably. A step stool is standard equipment for her, and having grown up with one always around, I've become accustomed to their usefulness. There's always something you need to reach that's just inches out of your grasp. If there are children in your life, a step stool helps bring your house into scale for them. The joinery—pegged bridle joints and half-laps—makes for a very rugged stool.

OAK STEP STOOL CUT LIST

- ▶ ⅜" × 12" oak dowel rod
- ▶ Sandpaper (120-, 180-grit)
- ▶ Wood glue
- **1: 1 × 8 × 96"**
  quartersawn red oak*

*RED OAK is one of, if not the most,
common hardwoods. Any lumberyard
and most building centers carry it in premilled
(often shrink-wrapped) boards in all of the common
dimensional sizes. It is a hard and durable wood, with better-
than-average resistance to rot. The natural reddish tone makes it instantly recognizable, although it
can limit your options in staining and finishing. But it is an affordable and available hardwood option
that is worth spending some time working with.

QUICK TIP

Dowels versus Pegs

Wood doweling and dowel pins are different materials that
serve different purposes. Doweling is simply the round-milled
stock sold in a variety of precut lengths—usually from 12" to
48". You can buy dowels milled from several wood species
in standard diameters, from ³⁄₁₆" up to 1½", including the red
oak seen here. In joinery, doweling is cut into "pegs" that are
driven completely through a joint and are often intended to
have their ends exposed for visual design purposes. Because
a peg (also called a through dowel) is visible on both sides
of a joint, the glue has a way to escape, so the peg does not
need to be fluted. Dowel pins are fluted, however, to allow
excess glue to escape while you're pressing the joint together.
They are meant solely to reinforce wood joints and are almost
never exposed. If they weren't fluted, the glue trapped inside
the joint could prevent the joint from fully seating.

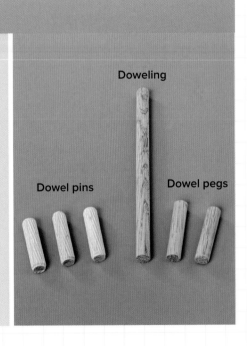

Doweling

Dowel pins

Dowel pegs

STEP STOOL CUT LIST

Overall Dimensions: 9" H × 12" D × 10" W

KEY	QTY	PART NAME	DIMENSION	MATERIAL
A	1	Top	¾" × 7½" × 10"	Oak
B	4	Frame Leg	¾" × 1½" × 10"	Oak
C	2	Frame Top	¾" × 1½" × 10"	Oak
D	2	Frame Bottom	¾" × 1½" × 12"	Oak
E	1	Stretcher	¾" × 1½" × 10"	Oak

The mortise-and-tenon joint between the Frame Leg and Top is pinned with a peg made from ⅜" doweling.

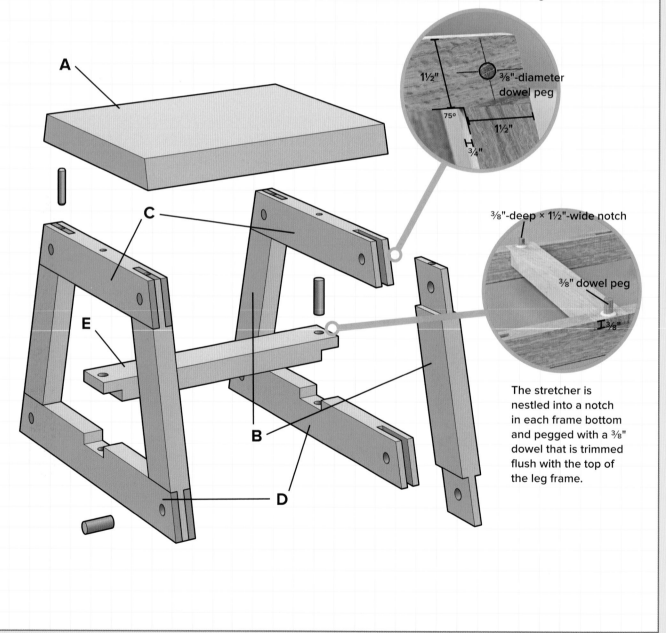

1½"   ⅜"-diameter dowel peg

75°   1½"

¾"

⅜"-deep × 1½"-wide notch

⅜" dowel peg

⅜"

The stretcher is nestled into a notch in each frame bottom and pegged with a ⅜" dowel that is trimmed flush with the top of the leg frame.

How to Build a Step Stool

STEP 1: Cut the stool top, slightly oversize if you have enough stock, from either a single 1 × 8" board (actual size is ¾" ×7½" although these days some premilled 1 × 8s are as narrow as 7¼") or by edge-gluing two narrower boards together, using biscuits or dowels to reinforce (see page 140). If the top is slightly oversized you can fit it to the assembled frame then sand it down to fit the frame perfectly.

STEP 2: Cut the leg frame parts to rough length. If you have purchased premilled 1 × 2", the stock should already be ¾" × 1½", so you do not need to do any planing or dimensioning. I cut the workpieces slightly longer than their planned finished lengths, and then cut all the angled ends and then trimmed them to length. The ends of all parts should be cut at a 75° angle—a power miter saw is the best tool for this, or you can use a miter box.

STEP 3: Cut the bridle joints and lapped stretcher joints in the frame parts using a table saw and a tenoning jig (see page 27 for details on modifying your tenoning jig to safely cut these angled joints. Also see pages 58–63 for more information on bridle joints). These are essentially open mortise-and-tenon joints and can also be hand-cut with a handsaw and wood chisel if you are not using a table saw.

STEP 4: Cut the stretcher to length and then cut the "tenons" at the ends of the stretcher by removing a ⅜ × ¾" section of waste from the bottom of each end.

STEP 5: Cut the ⅜ × 1½" notches that correspond to the stretcher tenons in the tops of the frame bottoms. Test-fit the joints and adjust by sanding or chiseling if needed until the top of the stretcher is flush with the tops of the frame bottoms.

STEP 6: Drill the ⅜"-diameter guide holes for the dowel pegs that will be driven through the joints between the stretcher and the bottom frame pieces (do this now, as you won't have clearance to drill them after the legs are assembled).

STEP 7: Assemble the legs using wood glue and spring clamps.

FEATURED TOOLS

Sliding T-Bevel

The sliding T-bevel is an indispensable tool for transferring angles. It's infinitely adjustable to any angle. Here, I use it to accurately take the angle for the tenon shoulders from the end of the leg part and transfer it to my miter gauge.

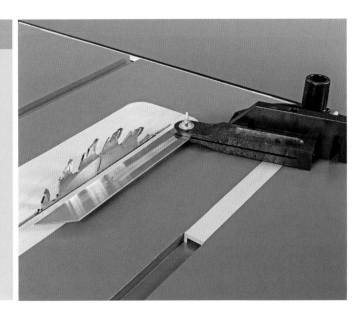

Once assembled, the ends of the frame tops should continue the lines of the frame legs.

STEP 8: When the glue is dry, drill holes through the joints for the dowel pegs. Cut the pegs to length, making them long enough to be just proud of both surfaces when installed. Apply glue to the pegs and tap them home with a mallet. Sand the ends of the pegs flush.

STEP 9: Glue the stretcher in place and drive in the glued pegs through the dowel guide holes at the joints. Trim or sand these pegs as you did the other pegs.

STEP 10: Set your table saw's blade at a 75° angle and then cut the top to finished size. You may also position the top board onto the leg assembly and extend the lines of the leg assembly onto the edges of the top board. Trim with a jigsaw and sand smooth so the top fits perfectly and continues the leg lines.

STEP 11: Drill dowel holes in the tops of the leg assemblies and then place the top upside down on a protected surface. Using dowel centers (see page 69), position the base on the underside of the top, and then press down to locate the dowel holes in the top.

STEP 11: Drill the ⅜"-diameter dowel holes in the underside of the top using a stop block to prevent drilling through. Glue in the ⅜"-diameter dowel pins and then glue and clamp the top to the legs. Complete the project by sanding, working your way up to 220-grit. Apply a finish of your choice.

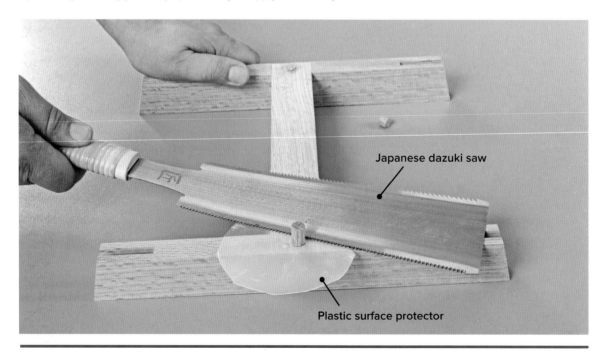

Japanese dazuki saw

Plastic surface protector

If the dowels stand ⅛" or more proud of the surface, I like to cut them close using a handsaw with a flexible blade (a *dozuki* Japanese saw is shown here), and then finish up using a sharp chisel or block plane. To make sure that the saw's teeth don't dig into the material, I cut a hole in a piece of plastic and slip it over the dowel.

Cutting Angled Bridle Joints

First, cut the angled parts. You'll use the tenoning jig for this procedure. Remove the 90° backing fence from the jig, and then cut another fence that has the same angle on one end as the pieces you're joining. Screw this angled backing fence to the jig's tall fence. Make the similar cuts at one setting before moving the fence. Cut the tenon cheeks using the tenoning jig. Use a miter gauge to cut the tenon shoulders.

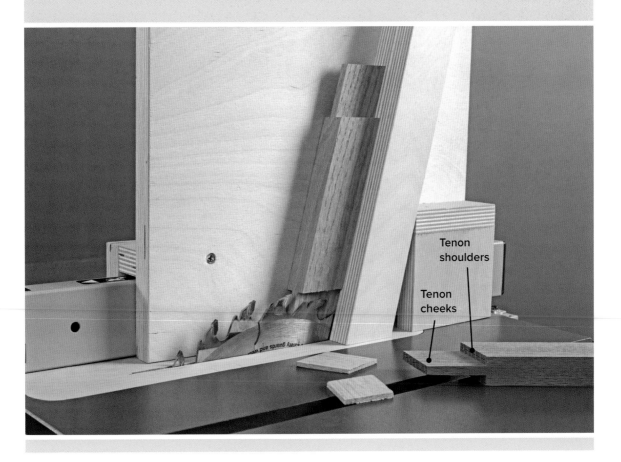

Tenon shoulders

Tenon cheeks

Frame-Leg Bench

Box joints and veneer make for cool, contemporary seating

What better way to make an impression on visitors than with a welcoming, on-trend bench placed near your entry door? This simple but sturdy bench offers a comfortable place for visitors and family members to be seated while they remove shoes or perhaps wait for a ride to arrive. You can put this handsome bench anywhere you like to provide overflow seating and a slick addition to your home décor.

Slender leg frames with box joints and hardwood veneer on the bench top set this entryway bench apart. Box joints look nice, but they aren't just decorative. Their purpose is to add mechanical strength and increase gluing surface. If you're not up for doing box joints, you can use a dowel joint instead. And by using veneer, you can transform layers of inexpensive MDF (medium density fiberboard) to resemble an expensive, chunky slab of hardwood. Don't be put off by veneering—using adhesive-backed veneer is almost as easy as putting on a sticker, and it holds up to regular use very well.

FRAME-LEG BENCH SHOPPING LIST

A dense hardwood like this African mahogany provides the structural integrity needed for bench legs, with the added benefit of deep, rich wood tones. For this entryway bench you will also need MDF to make the three-layer bench top substrate and a light-toned veneer (I used maple). A coat of sanding sealer prior to the veneer application improves the holding power.

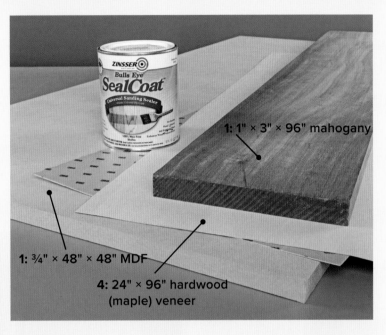

1: 1" × 3" × 96" mahogany

1: ¾" × 48" × 48" MDF

4: 24" × 96" hardwood (maple) veneer

Wood glue

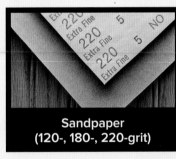

Sandpaper (120-, 180-, 220-grit)

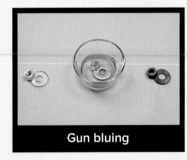

Gun bluing

Wood finish (light mahogany stain for legs, clear topcoat for all parts)

4: ⁵⁄₁₆" washers

4: ⁵⁄₁₆" × 3" lag screws

FRAME-LEG BENCH CUT LIST

Overall Dimensions: 17" H × 14" D × 40" W

KEY	QTY	PART NAME	DIMENSION	MATERIAL
A	3	Top	¾" × 15" × 40"	MDF
B	4	Leg	1" × 2½" × 17"	Mahogany
C	2	Foot	1" × 2½" × 15"	Mahogany

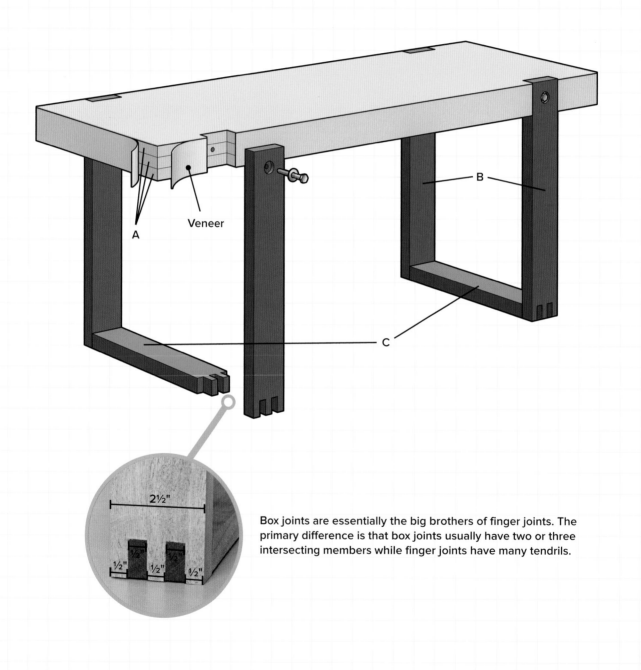

Veneer

A

B

C

2½"

½" ½" ½" ½"

Box joints are essentially the big brothers of finger joints. The primary difference is that box joints usually have two or three intersecting members while finger joints have many tendrils.

How to Build a Frame-Leg Bench

STEP 1: The bench top is made of three pieces of 14 × 40", ¾"-thick MDF. It is heavy and will last pretty much forever. It is also not much to look at unless you paint it, so I covered it with wood veneer. The effect is that it has the appearance of an impressive, thick slab of hardwood. Start by cutting the MDF pieces to size. A table saw makes short work of this since you can set the saw up for one cut and then make three identical cuts. But if you are careful, it is pretty easy to cut three identical workpieces with a circular saw and cutting guide (see page 127). Cut the three pieces of MDF for the seat to size.

STEP 2: Face-glue the seat pieces together. Clean them thoroughly first with a tack cloth to remove any dust or particles that could inhibit contact. Apply glue to two mating surfaces, press them together, and then add the third.

STEP 3: After the glue has dried (give it 24 hours), check to make sure all the edges are exactly flush. If there is variance, set the glue-up on edge and sand the edges with a belt sander until the edges are flush and square.

The bench top is notched to house the legs. Mark the locations of the 1"-deep by 2½"-wide leg notches on the bench top. Use a try square or speed square to extend the cutting lines across the edges of the bench top.

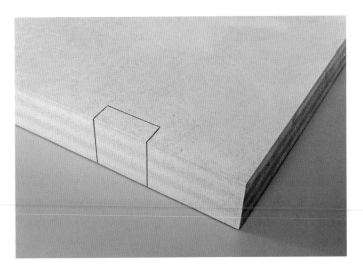

STEP 4: After cleaning the bench top workpiece, apply a thin coat of sanding sealer to the MDF surfaces to ensure a long-lasting bond with the veneer.

STEP 5: Cut the notches for the legs into the bench top. There are several ways to do this—the basic idea is to use a table saw or circular saw to remove most of the waste wood and then clean the edges of the notch with a wood chisel.

To make the leg cutouts, cut the shoulders first, and then make multiple passes in between with a table saw or circular saw. Clean out the waste with a sharp wood chisel.

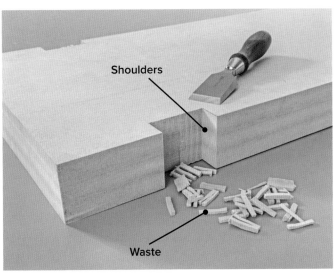

Shoulders

Waste

QUICK TIP

Veneer Sanding Block

Notches with broad bottoms need to be perfectly square or you will quickly see the inconsistencies. Here is a great device for smoothing out the notches to make sure they are square. If your notches match a common belt sander width, cut some scrap wood to that width so it fits snugly into the sanding belt. Wrap the belt around the wood and then use it as a sanding block to square up your notches.

STEP 6: Apply wood veneer to the bench top. Traditionally, wood veneer is purchased in sheets around $\frac{1}{64}$" thick and bonded to a substrate with contact cement. Recently, however, new self-adhesive veneer products offer an easier, more foolproof bonding strategy. I used self-adhesive maple veneer. Whether you are using self-adhesive veneer or traditional contact-glued material, apply the veneer to the edges of the bench top first and then the top. Let the edge veneer set and then line it up flush with the top surface of the bench top. Apply the top surface veneer, overlaying the top edges of the bench veneer by at least one inch. Trim the top veneer around the edges using a laminate trimmer or utility knife. You don't need to veneer the underside of the seat. For details on applying adhesive-backed veneer, see below.

Self-adhesive wood veneer sheets have made it easier than ever to apply veneer that holds to the substrate and lasts a long time. I like to cut the strips to size with a sharp scissors, but a sharp utility knife works, too. Cut and attach the edge strips first and then attach the veneer on the bench top surface.

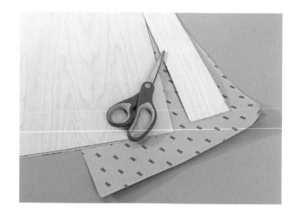

Self-adhesive veneer is easy to apply. You simply peel off the backing, position it, and roll it with a J-roller to set it. Trim the tops and bottoms of the veneer on the edges so the top veneer will overlay the edges of the bench top and the bottoms of the veneer strips are flush with the bottom of the bench top workpiece.

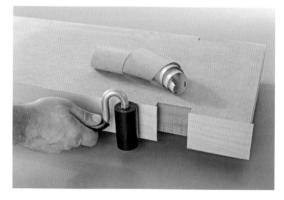

Trim off the excess veneer using a sharp chisel, utility knife, or veneer trimmer. Apply veneer to the remaining edges in the same manner. With all the edges veneered, trim the top surface to make sure all the veneer edges are flush. I recommend using a sanding block or veneer trimmer for this, and be careful not to sand in a direction that could pull the veneer off. Use the same method to apply the remaining visible surfaces. After all the surfaces are veneered and the waste trimmed, sand the corners using 150-grit paper. Sand just until the corners are smooth to the touch, being careful not to sand through the veneer.

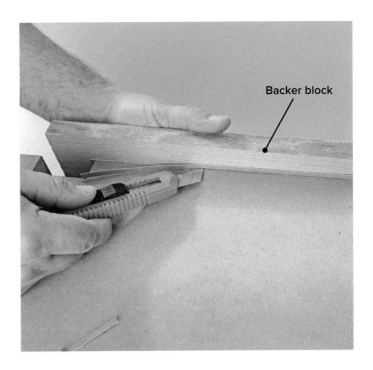

Backer block

STEP 7: Sand the veneered seat, working up with progressively finer sandpaper to 220-grit. Once it is perfect, move on to making the legs.

STEP 8: The legs are created by joining horizontal and vertical hardwood boards into two U-shaped parts. Cut the legs (the vertical members) and feet (the horizontal members) to final dimensions. How you accomplish this depends on what tools you have available—a table saw (to rip to width) and a power miter saw will do the job quickly and accurately, but a circular saw and straightedge guide and some handsaws will get you there, too.

STEP 9: The legs and feet are joined together with box joints. You could use dowel joints to reinforce these parts if you prefer (see page 114 for details on how to make a box joint jig). Cut box joints to connect the legs to the feet using a shop-made box joint jig.

STEP 10: Assemble the box joints to form two U-shaped legs, using glue and clamps. Check the leg assemblies for square. Sand the legs, starting with 120-grit, working your way up to 220-grit.

STEP 11: Predrill the tops of the leg assemblies in preparation for attaching them to the seat. Drill the counterbores for the lag screw heads and washers so the screw heads will be below the leg surface. Then, drill the clearence holes the rest of the way through the legs and pilot holes into the seat recesses.

STEP 12: Attach the legs to the seat using glue and lag screws with washers. I like to color the metal fasteners first using gun bluing (see page 95). Apply a finish of your choice.

Box Joint Jig

You can buy a box joint jig, but making your own is easy and inexpensive. Install a dado blade set to the exact thickness of the fingers you want to cut. Clamp a length of plywood or MDF to your double miter gauge fence (see page 97), and make a notch through it. Rip a piece of hardwood the exact size of the notch you just made. In this case, that piece is ½" wide and ¾" tall. Cut off a short piece for the jig's pin, and then glue it into the notch. Keep the remaining length of the hardwood strip as a spacer.

Clamp the jig onto your fence again using the spacer to locate the pin exactly ½" to the right of the dado set. Locate your stock against the pin and make a cut. Slip that cut over the pin and make the next cut. Continue this process to cut the rest of the joints. Slip the last notch over the pin as a spacer, and then cut the joints in the mating piece just as you did the first one.

The width of the stock you're cutting joints in needs to be an exact multiple of the width of the pin, so that the joints come out evenly. Start with scrap pieces that are the exact dimension of the stock you'll be using. If the joint comes out a little off, shift the jig a tiny increment left or right, and then cut another test joint. Continue testing until the joint comes out perfectly.

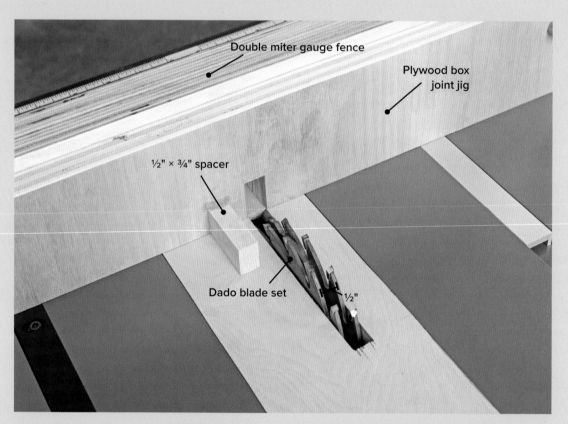

Double miter gauge fence

Plywood box joint jig

½" × ¾" spacer

Dado blade set

½"

To make a box joint jig for your table saw, start by ripping a piece of wood (plywood is a good choice) to the same width as your double miter gauge fence (see page 97) and then clamp the plywood to the miter gauge fence. Install a dado blade set in your saw and adjust it to match the thickness and depth of the notches you are cutting (here, ½" wide and ¾" deep). Cut a notch in the plywood. Fit a ½" × ¾" spacer into the notch to use as a spacing guide.

Slide the leg against the pin and cut the first notch. Slip the notch over the pin and cut the second notch. Secure the workpiece to the jig and feed it through the dado blade set to cut the adjoining notch.

Slip the last notch from the first board over the pin. The last "finger" becomes the spacer to start cutting the mating notches on the second board.

Round End Table

This delicate but sturdy end table features some refined router work and elegant tapered legs.

A perfect spot for a beverage or a book, this table's tapered legs give it a light and refined look. I chose two species that complement each other nicely—maple and walnut—but you could make this from a single species as well. A shop-made jig for the table saw makes quick work of the tapered legs. You'll also learn how to make a special baseplate for your router to cut perfect circles. In the end, you will have a versatile home furnishing that can fit in just about anywhere you ask it to.

ROUND END TABLE SHOPPING LIST

Walnut and maple are common but lovely hardwoods. They can be purchased in premilled dimensions—for this project, you can buy 8' lengths of 2 × 2 and 1 × 6 of walnut and a ½" × 4' piece of maple. Or if you have the right tools you can mill your own parts from random-width stock purchased at a lumberyard.

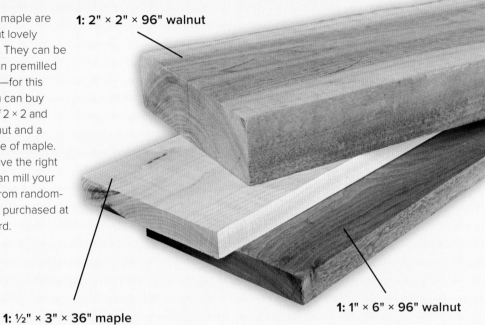

1: 2" × 2" × 96" walnut

1: ½" × 3" × 36" maple

1: 1" × 6" × 96" walnut

▶ **Joinery biscuits**　▶ **Sanding belt**

Wood glue

Sandpaper (120-, 180-, 220-grit)

Wood finish

1½" × 1½" L-brackets

ROUND END TABLE CUT LIST

Overall Dimensions: 21¼" H × 18" D × 18" W

KEY	QTY	PART NAME	DIMENSION	MATERIAL
A	4	Leg	1½" × 1½" × 20"	Walnut
B	2	Cross Pieces	½" × 2" × 18"	Maple
C	1	Top	¾" × 17" × 17"	Walnut

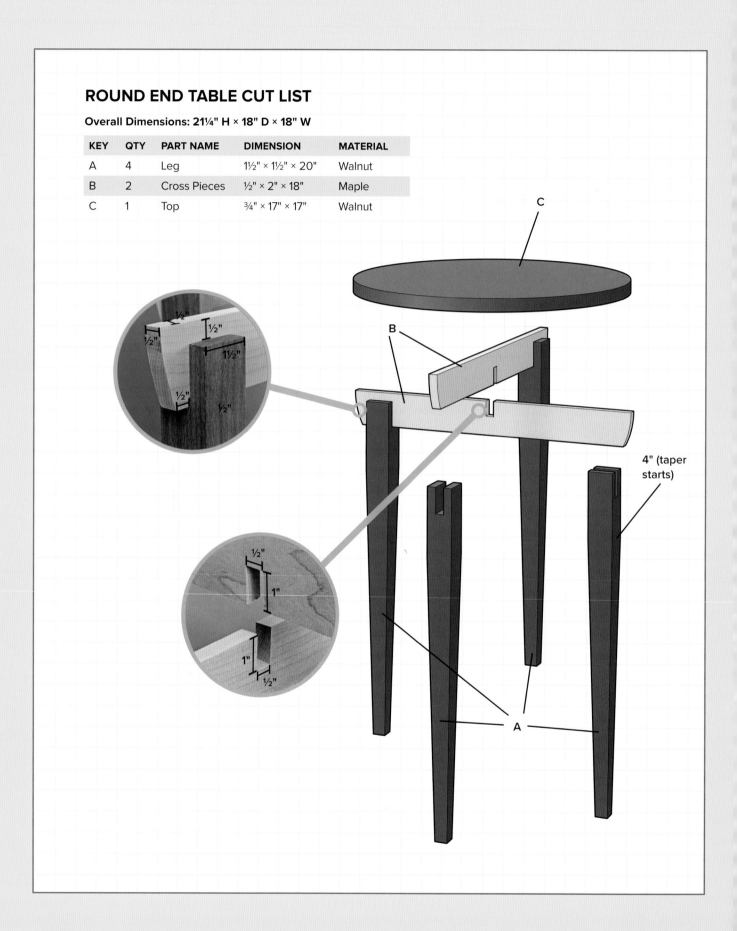

4" (taper starts)

How to Build a Round End Table

STEP 1: Start by making the maple crosspieces that support the tabletop. Although ½"-thick stock can be harder to find at building centers than standard ¾"-thick wood, they look more proportional. Acquire or mill stock to ½ × 3" and cut to finished length (18").

STEP 2: Cut ½"-wide by 1"-deep notches in the center of each crosspiece so they will mate together to form a half-lap joint. A table saw and dado blade set work well for this (see page 51) or you can cut the notch shoulders with a handsaw, remove the waste, and clean up the shoulders and bottoms of the notches with a wood chisel. Test the fit to make sure the parts are flush on the tops when the half-lap joint is made.

STEP 3: Lay out a gentle curve at both ends of each crosspiece, starting at the top and curving down to a point at the bottom ½" from the end of the part. For consistency, cut one end with a jigsaw and then sand it until the curve is smooth and even. Use this profile as a guide for cutting the other three ends. Then, break the edges of the end profiles by making a chamfer cut with a hand plane.

Cut the curves on the support ends using a jigsaw and then sand to the line. Give the sharp corners a slight chamfer using a block plane or sanding block.

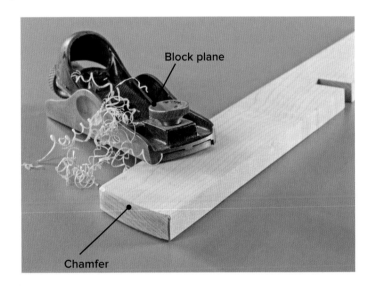

Block plane

Chamfer

STEP 4: Cut a "blank" for each leg, 1½ × 1½ × 20".

STEP 5: The finished legs are tapered from top to bottom beginning 4" down. When you are cutting tapers, it is best to make any other cuts you need before you make the tapers as the workpiece will no longer be square for registering the parts. Each of these table legs is milled with a ½"-wide by 1 ½"-deep notch in the top end to house the maple crosspieces. A table saw and tenoning jig (see page 27) are good for making these cuts, otherwise use a handsaw and chisel. Cut the notches in all four leg blanks.

STEP 6: Cutting tapers is difficult if you do not have access to a table saw, especially if you are working with parts as small as these leg blanks. If you have access to a table saw, use a tenoning jig (see page 27) on a table saw to cut the top slots that house the crosspieces. The tapers should begin 4" down from the top of each leg, removing ⅜" from each face of the blank. This results in a leg that is ¾" wide on the bottom and 1½" wide on top. Taper the legs on all four sides using a tapering jig on the table saw.

Four-Sided Taper

To make long tapers on four sides, use a tapering jig. As long as you have a flat section at the top of the legs, you can taper three sides, no problem. But for the fourth side, the underside of the leg is unsupported, which is dangerous. To remedy this, use double-faced tape to fasten an offcut from one of the other sides as a shim underneath the unsupported portion.

An adjustable tapering jig can be used and reused to cut tapers of many angles with your table saw.

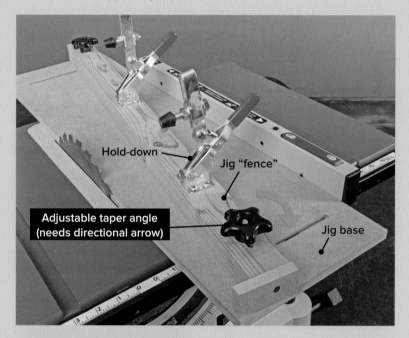

Hold-down

Jig "fence"

Adjustable taper angle (needs directional arrow)

Jig base

When using a tapering jig, clamp down the workpiece against the jig fence and cut the tapers on two adjoining sides of each piece. Reserve the cutoff pieces and use them as shims with the already-tapered sides so they ride cleanly and safely against the table and the jig fence.

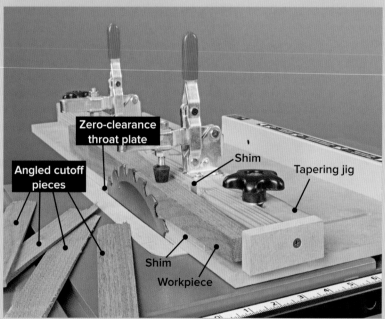

Zero-clearance throat plate

Shim

Tapering jig

Angled cutoff pieces

Shim

Workpiece

STEP 7: Glue the maple crosspieces into opposing legs and let the glue dry. Then, glue the leg/crosspiece assemblies together at the half-lap.

Glue the legs/crosspiece assemblies together and check for square.

STEP 8: Make the tabletop. In most cases, you'll need to edge-glue one or more pieces of hardwood stock to create a workpiece that is wide enough (minimum 18 × 18"). See pages 91-93 for more information on edge-gluing. Edge-glue the tabletop boards. After the glue is dry, sand the top smooth.

STEP 9: Trim the tabletop workpiece into a circular shape. There are several ways to do this: I used a router and a circle-cutting jig (see below). You can also rough-cut the circle shape using a jigsaw, and then sand to the line with a stationary belt sander (see page 67).

STEP 10: Sand the base and the top, breaking over any sharp edges. Apply a finish of your choice. I used clear varnish.

STEP 11: Set the tabletop upside down on a flat surface and attach the leg/crosspiece assembly. Use 1½" × 1½" L-brackets (one per leg) to attach the top. Be sure to predrill your screw holes in all parts.

QUICK TIP

Routing a Perfect Circle

To rout a perfect circle, make a baseplate for your router from ¼"-thick hardboard. This baseplate extends out to the side, so you can make a pivot point using a nail. By rotating your router around that point, it will cut a perfect circle. Always try to do this from the underside of a workpiece, to avoid making a visible nail hole in the visible surface. After attaching the baseplate to your workpiece's center using a nail, you're ready to start routing.

Rout the circle in stages with a straight-cutting bit, increasing the depth of cut by a maximum of ³⁄₁₆" at a time until the cut is complete.

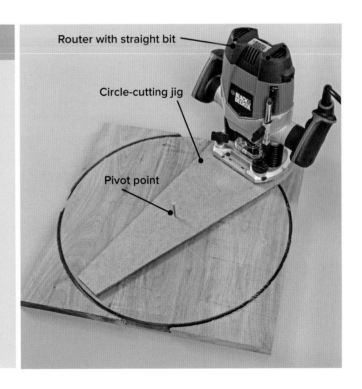

Router with straight bit

Circle-cutting jig

Pivot point

Sliding Barn Door

Turn extra tongue-and-groove flooring into an eye-catching door

If you have a room in your house where a conventional swinging door seems like it's always in the way, or you're just looking for a change, consider a sliding barn door. This type of door slides on a track like a pocket door, but instead of disappearing into a wall cavity it moves to the side where it remains visible. A quick Internet search will reveal many types of barn door hardware available. You could also visit a salvage yard and make an adventure of finding your hardware.

I decided to make this door a little less barn-doorish; since the back of the door is OSB—a typical material for a subfloor—I decided on flooring for the door's face. It'll be great practice if you ever want to install an actual floor, and I'll also show you a slick technique for making perfectly straight cuts on large pieces, such as sheets of plywood, using a circular saw. The door I made is 40¾" wide by 90¾" tall—considerably larger than a standard 32- or 36" × 80" door opening. Adjust the door's dimensions to fit your doorway.

SLIDING BARN DOOR SHOPPING LIST

- ▶ 1½" utility screws
- ▶ Flooring adhesive
- ▶ Wood putty
- ▶ Wood glue
- ▶ Wood finish
- ▶ Finish nails

Walnut

Maple

Walnut

6" wide (5½" actual) bamboo flooring. 40 square feet tongue-and-groove flooring*

1: ¾" OSB

Barn door hardware**

*TONGUE-AND-GROOVE FLOORING is not just for floors. The same forgiveness in wood movement provided by the joinery method makes for a solid floor, but also is an advantage to other applications where motion and changes in temperature and humidity can create havoc. That's one reason why I chose to use flooring product to clad this sliding barn door. In this case, I had a few dozen square feet of leftover prefinished bamboo flooring that had been sitting in a shed for ten years or so. Not quite enough for a floor, but too lovely to waste. Bamboo flooring is created by gluing long strands of bamboo together under pressure. It is hard and durable with a unique exotic appearance, and because bamboo grows so quickly, it is highly renewable. An OSB subbase mainly adds weight/ballast, but also provides a surface for attaching the flooring.

**I used Rockler brand hardware; this is set #59088.

SLIDING BARN DOOR CUT LIST

Overall Dimensions: 90¾" H × 1½" D × 40¾" W

KEY	QTY	PART NAME	DIMENSION	MATERIAL
A	1	Back	¾" × 40" × 90"	OSB
B	32 sq. ft.	Door Face	¾" × 4"	Bamboo Flooring
C	24 lineal feet	Edging	⅜" × 1½"	Bamboo

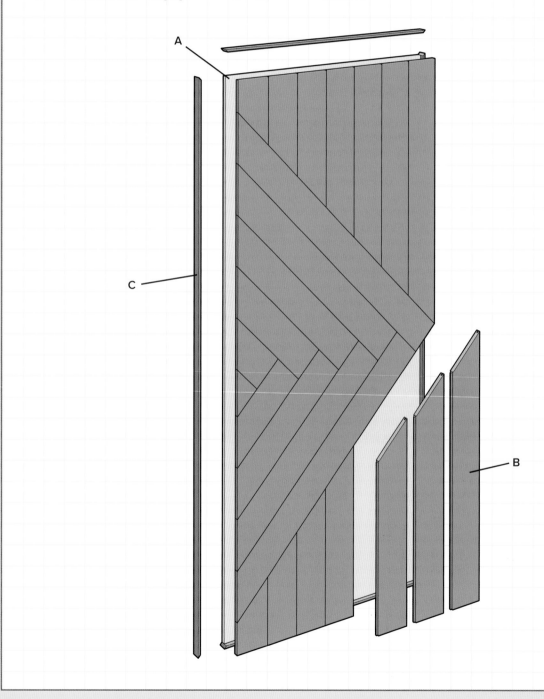

How to Build a Sliding Barn Door

STEP 1: Lay out the door's outer dimension on the back side of the OSB and then draw the flooring pattern.

Outline the dimensions of the door on the substrate and then draw reference lines to establish the diagonal pattern.

STEP 2: Set up a pair of sawhorses on a flat floor, and fasten three straight 2 × 4s to them, on edge—one along each edge, and one down the center.

STEP 3: Cut the first long center flooring piece using the pattern layout and outer dimension marks to calculate its length. Leave it a bit long. You'll cut the door to size later.

STEP 4: Cut, glue, and nail the herringbone pattern boards in place. You don't need to glue the tongue-and-groove joints, but do glue the ends where they butt against the previous board.

Drill angled pilot holes through the tongue and then glue and nail the board in place.

Before nailing the first board in place, trim the tongue off the end where the next board butts into it. Make this cut on each board in the herringbone section before installing it.

Mitered corners give the edging a
cleaner look. Pin the miter joints with
finish nails to help keep the miters
from opening up.

STEP 5: Working from the long sides,
cut, glue, and fasten the vertical pieces in
place. Check the distance to your layout
marks as you go to make sure the flooring
is staying square.

STEP 6: Cut the door to final size using a
circular saw with a guide (see next page).

STEP 7: Rip ⅜"-thick strips of flooring for
the door edging. Attach the door edging
using glue and finish nails. You can miter
the corners or use butt joints.

STEP 8: Fill the nail holes in the edging
with wood putty, sand, and then apply a
finish of your choice.

The edges of the floorboard pattern
and substrate should be square and
flush after trimmning.

QUICK TIP

Miter Saw Setup

Leave your miter saw set at the correct angle and cut the boards to rough length using a handsaw or
circular saw. This way, you don't have to keep resetting your miter saw.

FEATURED TOOLS

Circular Saw Cutting Guide

Cutting large pieces on a tablesaw is cumbersome at best and dangerous at worst. You can make perfectly straight cuts using a shop-made cutting guide for your saw. You'll need a sheet of ¼"-thick tempered hardboard and a sheet of foam insulation. Set the sheet of hardboard on the insulation, and then rip a strip 5½" wide. Mark the factory edge, as that will be your fence. Cut another strip 11" wide for the base. Glue the fence on top of the base, with the factory edge at the center of the base. When the glue is dry, set the assembly on the foam insulation. Make a cut with the edge of your saw's baseplate held firmly against the factory edge of the fence, ripping off the outer edge of the base. To use the jig, mark your cuts, clamp the jig on your workpiece with the freshly cut edge on your marks, and make the cut. Make two or three guides of different lengths.

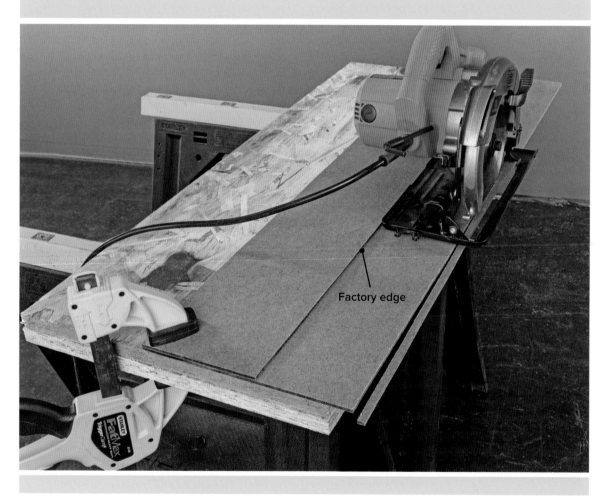

Factory edge

Cross-Leg Desk

Simple lines and a refined design offer a generous worksurface in a small footprint.

Strong joinery and sturdy stock means you can create furnishings that step out of the clunky mode you tend to find in most homemade projects. For this desk I used ipe, an exotic hardwood used primarily for decking, to make the legs. Ipe is very dense and strong, which makes it ideal for leg stock. On the joinery front, this desk uses half-laps, like other projects in this book. The only difference is that in this case the mating parts are angled. That might seem more difficult, but like any other joint, you're just cutting a line on a board. If you're careful in your layout, it's just as straightforward.

The desktop is fashioned from a double layer of Baltic birch plywood. Baltic birch is known for its clear surfaces and void-free lamination layers. Beveled edges on the side of the top make it look sleeker to the eye.

CROSS-LEG DESK SHOPPING LIST

¾" × 60" × 60" Baltic birch (1)

⁴⁄₄-thick × 96"-long ipe*
(enough to rip-cut into
three 2"-wide strips)

* **IPE** is a Brazilian hardwood called prized for its durability and weather resistance. It is very popular for deck boards and railings, so it's generally available at home centers (although often it is a special order product). A typical ipe deck board is nominal ⁵⁄₄ x 6", with actual dimensions of 1" thick by 5½" wide. Because the deck boards have bullnose edges, there will be some waste to achieve the square corners you'll want on all parts" meaning, you'll only be able to get two 2"-wide strips out of a deck bard. Dense and heavy, ipe has very small wood pores, so some wood finishing materials with larger molecular structures do not penetrate it well. Look for finishes rated for exotic hardwoods. Ipe is also very oily and its sawdust can be an irritant, so always wear protective gear when working with it.

1½" wood screws

▶ Wood glue
▶ Wood finish

CROSS-LEG DESK CUT LIST

Overall Dimensions: 28½" H x 23¼" D x 41" W

KEY	QTY	PART NAME	DIMENSION	MATERIAL
A	4	Leg	1" x 2" x 36"	Ipe
B	4	Plates	1" x 2" x 18"	Ipe
C	1	Foot Rail	1" x 2" x 40"	Ipe
D	2	Top	¾" x 23¼" x 41"	Baltic Birch

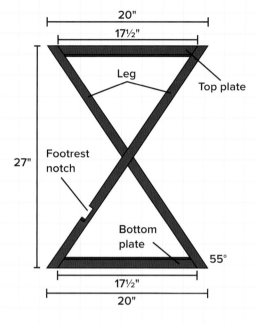

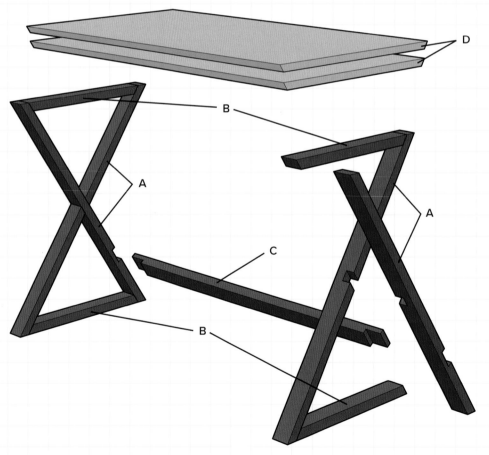

How to Build a Cross-Leg Desk

STEP 1: Cut the ipe (or other hardwood of your choice) stock for the legs and footrest to rough length. All parts should be the same width and thickness (although you can fudge it a bit on the footrest if you need to). A typical ipe deck board is listed as ⁵⁄₄" but the actual thickness is 1" (⁴⁄₄). If you are using premilled wood that is not decking, look for stock that is at least a full 1" thick. If you have a tablesaw, rip-cut the stock to width, or use a circular saw and straightedge cutting guide (see page 127). Because the wood is so dense, you'll want a ripping blade to get a clean, smooth cut without burning.

STEP 2: Make a full-size drawing or template to use as a guide for laying out the leg assembly (this is a big help when you're figuring out cutting angles). I used a scrap of MDF (medium-density fiberboard) cut to 20 × 27", making sure all the corners were exactly 90°. Trace one of the actual pieces of 1 × 2 stock onto the template to make your layout lines for the "X" created by the two legs. Then use the same piece of stock to trace layout lines for the plates that join the tops and bottoms of the legs. Because of the 55° angles formed at the tops and bottoms of the leg assemblies, the inside layout lines for the legs should be 17½" apart along the 20" sides of the template.

STEP 3: Lay the leg stock onto the template and mark cutoff lines on each end. By making these cutting lines with a mechanical transfer you avoid needing to rely on setting the 55° cutting angle on your saw. Cut the legs to length at the cutting lines, making sure the ends of each leg are parallel.

STEP 4: Lay the crossing pieces on the drawing again to mark the half-lap joints. TIP: Apply some masking tape to the workpieces at the joint location. Mark the points where the legs cross the mating legs on each face of each workpiece.

Lay out the entire joint on each piece and verify that all the joints are in the right orientation. Mark the waste areas onto tape you've applied to the legs.

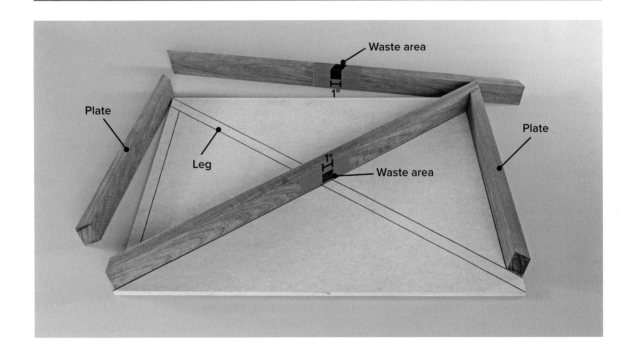

STEP 5: Cut the half-lap notch in each workpiece. If you have a tablesaw, use a miter gauge set to 55° (double-check against your actual angles) and set the blade cutting height to 1". If you are using a handsaw, such as a backsaw, secure the workpiece and carefully follow the cutting lines to cut the notch shoulders. Then, remove the waste material with a coping saw and use a sharp wood chisel to clean the bottom of each notch. Test the fit to make sure the edges of the legs are flush with one another when the joint is assembled.

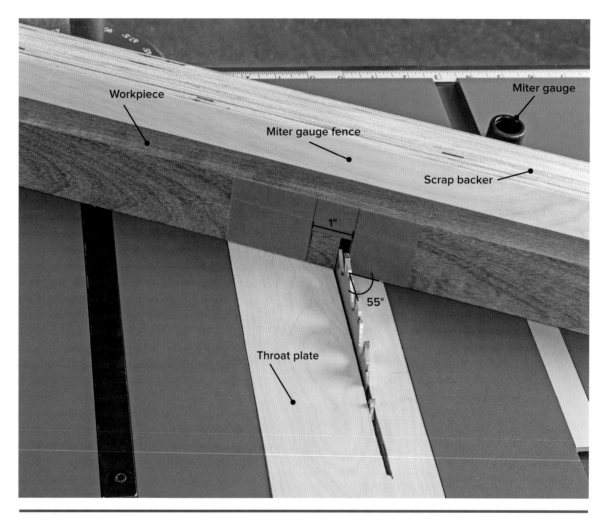

Cut the angled half-laps using a tablesaw and miter gauge with a scrap wood backer between the workpiece and the fence of the miter gauge. Remove all the waste in each notch, making multiple passes until you have reached 1" in width.

STEP 6: Lay out and cut the notches for the footrest. You'll notch both the legs and the footrest for this joint. The footrest notches in the legs should align exactly. In the legs, the notches should be ½" deep and perpendicular to the legs. In the footrest, remove a ½"-thick by 1"-long section at each end. Use a tablesaw and tenoning jig if you have one (see page 27) or make the cuts with a handsaw or jigsaw and wood chisel.

**The wide notches in the legs (½" deep by 2")
will house the notched ends of the footrest. The
notches should be perpendicular to the legs,
starting approximately 7¼" up from the ends
of the legs. Make sure the notches in the two legs
are exactly aligned.**

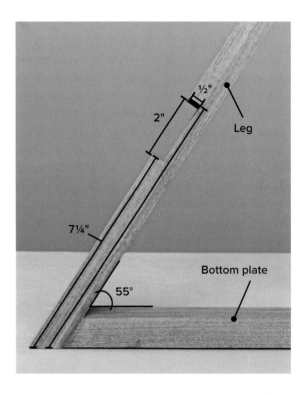

STEP 7: Assemble the two X-shaped legs. Apply glue to the angled half-lap joints and assemble the legs. Be sure the distance between the open ends of each "X" is the same at the top and bottom of the leg.

STEP 8: Allow the glue in the leg joints to dry and then lay each assembly on a flat worksurface. Position the stock for the top and bottom plates against the top and bottom of each leg assembly and trace cutting lines for the parts so they fit snugly between the leg ends. Check the parts against the plate layout lines on your template and then cut the plates to length using a miter saw.

STEP 9: Drill a pair of counterbored pilot holes through each plate end and into the mating leg end. Orient the pilot holes so the drill entry point is on the underside of the bottom plates and the top side of the top plates. TIP: Use a combination square to make sure the pilot hole is perpendicular to the faces of the legs. Glue the plates and attach them with screws.

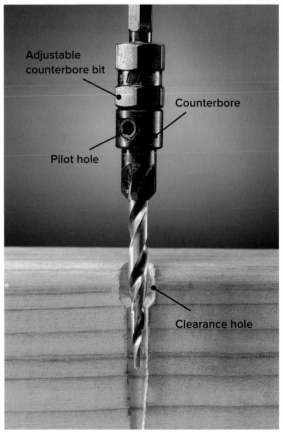

**TIP: Careful counterbores are critical in this
project. A true counterbore (contrast to simple
countersink holes) has three parts: a *pilot hole* to
full depth; a *clearance hole* that is slightly wider
to accommodate the thicker shank in the upper
area of a tapered wood screw; and the *counterbore*
itself, which is slightly larger than the diameter
of the screw head and has straight edges. You
can drill a three-part counterbore hole using
three differently sized drill bits, or you can use an
adjustable counterbore bit (right) that can drill
the hole in one pass.**

STEP 10: After the leg/plate assemblies have dried, join them by attaching the footrest in the leg notches, making sure the ends of the footrest are flush with the outside edges of the leg assemblies.

STEP 11: Cut the two desktop workpieces, slightly oversize, from Baltic birch plywood. Choose the clearest surface for the top piece, and then laminate the boards together with the top piece facing down on your worksurface. Use glue and screws driven from the bottom of the assembly to laminate the two boards together.

STEP 12: Cut the top to finished length and width using a circular saw and cutting guide. Cut 55° bevels on the long (front and back) edges of the desktop, using a tablesaw or a circular saw and cutting guide.

STEP 13: Sand all the parts, working your way up to 220-grit, and then apply a finish. Attach the top using countersunk screws through the top plates: three per end should be adequate. Do not glue the top/plate connection.

FEATURED SKILL

Angled Drilling

To drill at the proper angle, set a combination square across the joint. Hold the combination square in place on the workpiece as you're drilling as a visual guide.

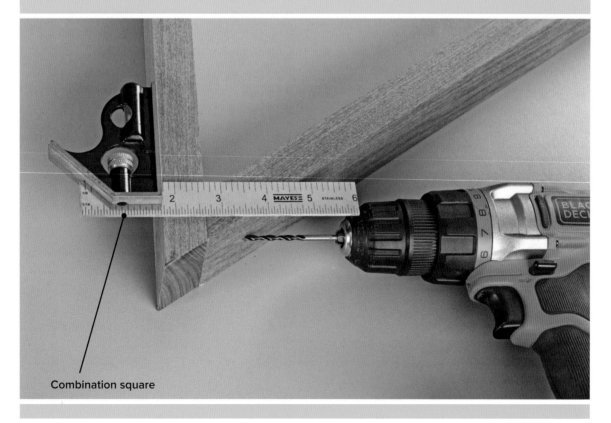

Combination square

QUICK TIP

Waxing Screws

Waxing a screw before driving helps the screw drive without breaking. This is particularly important in dense woods like ipe. A toilet wax ring provides a lifetime supply of screw lubricant.

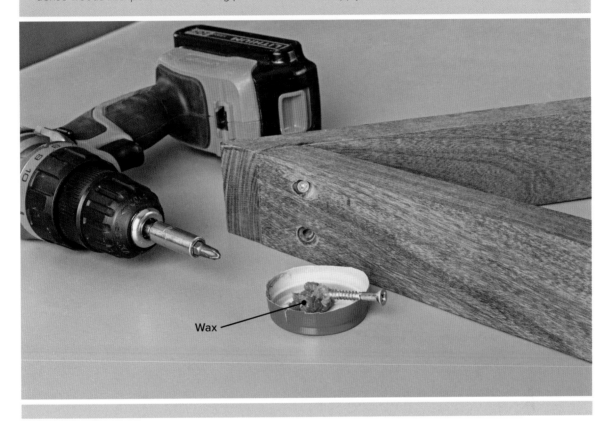

Wax

Nightstand with Drawer

A place for all your bedside essentials.

A good nightstand with a drawer is practically a necessity in modern life. And when you build it yourself from good-quality hardwood, it becomes as attractive as it is useful. This particular model, made from walnut with a maple drawer front as an accent, is relatively easy to make. Building the drawer is also not too difficult, and it's a great exercise to get some experience in drawer building.

Typically, good hardwood lumber purchased from a home center is surfaced on four sides, with two straight edges, so they're ready to use. If your lumber isn't exactly straight, I'll show you an easy method to straighten boards on the tablesaw to make good glue joints. I used walnut for this nightstand and added curly maple for the drawer face. You're not likely to find curly maple sold at the home center on purpose, but if you dig through the pile of maple, you might find some with really nice figure that made it there by accident. Otherwise, visit your local lumberyard. These species are a bit more expensive than the more common varieties typical in the construction trades, but for a small project like this, they won't break the bank.

NIGHTSTAND SHOPPING LIST

1: ½" × 3" × 13" maple (curly as shown)

1: 1" × 4" × 96" walnut
or 2" × 2"

▶ Walnut stock:
(1) 1" × 8" × 48"
or (1) 2" × 2" × 96"
and (1) 1" × 8" × 24"

1: ½" × 60" × 60"
Baltic birch plywood

1: ¼" × 2' × 2 ft. plywood

▶ Joinery biscuits

▶ ¼" dowels

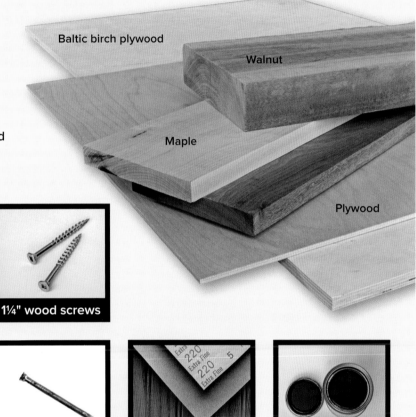

Baltic birch plywood

Walnut

Maple

Plywood

Wood glue

1¼" wood screws

2" finish nails

Sandpaper
(120-, 180-, 220-grit)

Wood finish

NIGHTSTAND WITH DRAWER CUT LIST

Overall Dimensions: 24½" H × 15" D × 22" W

KEY	QTY	PART NAME	DIMENSION	MATERIAL
A	1	Top	¾" × 15" × 22"	Walnut
B	4	Leg	1½" × 1½" × 24¼"	Walnut
C	2	Side	¾" × 4" × 9"	Walnut
D	1	Back	¾" × 4" × 13"	Walnut
E	2	Front Rails	¾" × ¾" × 13"	Walnut
F	2	Side Stretchers	¾" × 1" × 9"	Walnut
G	4	Drawer Guide	¾" × 1½" × 9"	Walnut
H	2	Drawer Slide	½" × ¾" × 9"	Walnut
I	2	Drawer Side	½" × 2⅞" × 9½"	Birch Plywood
J	1	Drawer Front	½" × 2⅞" × 12⅜"	Birch Plywood
K	1	Drawer Back	½" × 2⅜" × 12⅜"	Birch Plywood
L	1	Drawer Bottom	¼" × 9¼" × 12½"	Birch Plywood
M	1	Drawer Face	¾" × 2⅞" × 12⅞"	Curly Maple

How to Build a Nightstand with Drawer

STEP 1: Prepare the wood stock to make the top. In most cases that means edge-gluing two pieces of wood together to create a top that is wide enough (15" as shown). I used two pieces of walnut 1 × 8 (actual width 7 ½"). Cut the pieces for the top slightly overlong in length, and then use a jointer or a jointing plane to prepare the mating edges for edge-gluing (see page 140). If the top ends up slightly under or over the listed dimensions, that is fine, since the top overhangs the table base on all sides. Edge-glue the mating parts together using biscuits or dowels to align the parts and reinforce the joint. When the glue is dry, trim the top to finished length.

STEP 2: I cut chamfers into the bottom edges of the tabletop, mostly for visual reasons but also to minimize the head-banging hazard posed by corners. I used a tablesaw with the blade set to 30° to trim off the bottom ¼" of the top, all the way around. If you don't have a tablesaw you can use a router or (even more fun) build your hand tools skills by cutting the chamfers with a hand plane.

STEP 3: Sand the top, beginning with 80-grit sandpaper, working your way up to 180-grit. Ease all the sharp edges and then apply finish to all surfaces. Set the top aside.

STEP 4: To make the legs you'll need stock that is at least 1½ × 1½" thick. Most building centers probably do not carry walnut in this thickness, but if you can locate some 2 × 4 or 2 × 6 walnut at a lumberyard, you'll save a couple of steps. Otherwise, face-glue some ¾"-thick stock and then rip it to 1½"-wide strips on your tablesaw or with a circular saw and cutting guide. Cut the strips to leg length (the 23¾" length used here allow you to cut all four legs from a single 8'-long 2 × 2.

STEP 5: Cut the sides, back, front rails, and drawer glides and slides to size. As with the legs, rip-cut your stock to width first and then trim it to length.

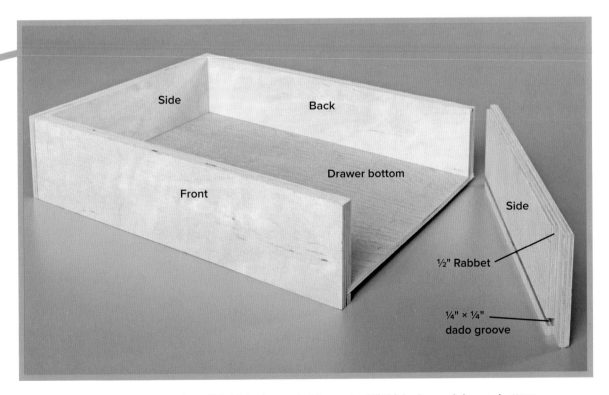

The drawer box is constructed from ½"-thick plywood sides and a ¼"-thick plywood drawer bottom.

Biscuit Jointer

A biscuit jointer (also called a plate jointer) is one of my favorite tools for ensuring the alignment of mating parts. It uses a small circular cutting blade to create a semicircular slot in which plates or biscuits are inserted during assembly. These biscuits not only help with alignment, but they also add a measure of strength.

To use a biscuit jointer, line up the parts and make a mark across the joint, to register the biscuit cutter on each piece. Line up the centering mark on the biscuit jointer's fence with the mark on each workpiece and cut the slot. When you're assembling the parts, make sure to get glue into the slots.

A biscuit jointer can be adjusted up and down for different material thicknesses. You can also adjust the depth of the slot for different-sized biscuits. You can use a biscuit jointer's fence to locate the slots, or you can register the biscuit jointer off of a flat surface with the fence folded up.

Use a biscuit jointer (plate jointer) and biscuits (or dowels) to help align the mating boards when edge-gluing the tabletop. The biscuits or dowels also help strengthen the joint somewhat, but alignment is their primary purpose.

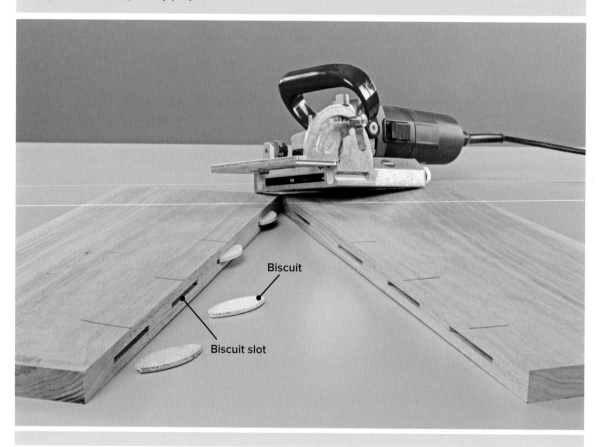

Biscuit

Biscuit slot

The bottom edges of the glued-up tabletop are chamfered at 30°. You can make the chamfer cuts with a tablesaw or try using a sharp hand plane to do the job.

STEP 6: Attach the sides, back, and front rails to the tops of the legs, using dowel joints (see page 38). Drill dowel holes in the ends of the sides, back, and front rails and then use dowel centers to mark drilling points for the mating drill holes in the legs. Drill their mating holes in the legs (use a drill press if you have one). Then, create the table base by gluing dowels in all the joints. Note: The joints for the sides and back are in parts that can manage a ⅜" dowel (you never want to remove more than half the thickness of the board). But use a pair of ¼"-diameter dowels to reinforce each front rail joint to avoid removing too much waste, which can cause the rails to split.

Use metal dowel centers to transfer the dowel hole locations from the sides and back onto the tops of the legs. Use a combination square set to ¼" as a guide for setting the reveal before pressing down on the dowel centers.

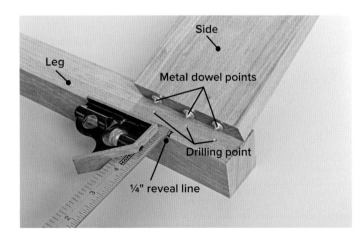

STEP 7: Cut the remaining table base parts (the drawer guides and slides) to width and length from the leftover walnut stock. Attach them to the inside faces of the table base sides with countersunk flathead wood screws (1¼")

The table base is assembled with ⅜" dowels to make the joints between the sides and back and the legs. The front rails are attached to the legs with one ¼" dowel per joint.

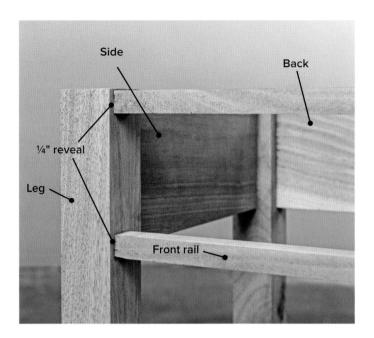

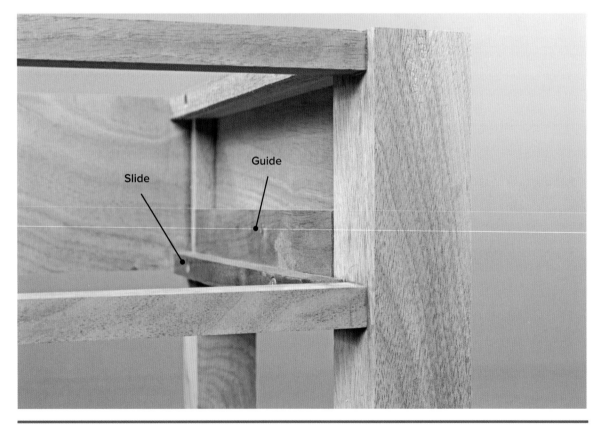

The drawer guides and slides are cut from leftover walnut stock.

STEP 8: The nightstand drawer is basically a plywood box with a chunk of maple attached to the front for appearance. There are many methods you can use for making drawers, from simple butt joints to box joints or finger joints. For this drawer, which gets relatively low usage and doesn't need to support a lot of weight, I cut simple rabbet joints into the ends of the drawer sides to house the ends of the box front and back. The sides and front are milled with a dado groove ½" up from the bottom edges to hold the plywood drawer bottom. The back of the box is left ½" narrower than the sides and front so the drawer bottom fits up against the bottom of the part. Cut the drawer box front, back and sides to size from ½" thick no-void plywood (I used Baltic birch).

STEP 9: Cut ½"-wide, ¼"-deep rabbets in the ends of the box sides, using a tablesaw and dado blade set (see page 51) or a router table.

STEP 10: Cut a ¼"-deep groove along the inside bottom edge of the two sides ½" up from the bottom edge. Cut the drawer bottom to dimensions from ¼" plywood—I used Baltic birch for this part, too.

STEP 11: Assemble the drawer box using glue and finish nails. Clamp the box and check for square, adjusting the clamps as necessary until square is achieved. Once the joints have dried, test the drawer's fit in the drawer opening and make any necessary adjustments using a sanding block or block plane.

STEP 12: Insert the drawer bottom panel into the channels in the bottom of the box frame. The fit should be just a little loose. Tack the drawer bottom to the underside of the box back with finish nails.

Slide the bottom into the groove and finish-nail it to the underside of the drawer's back.

STEP 13: Cut the drawer face to size; I used a piece of ¾"-thick maple. The drawer face should overhang the front of the drawer box by about ¹⁄₁₆" on all sides. Chamfer the edges with a sanding block or block plane. Sand the face and edges.

STEP 14: Attach the drawer face. Drill and countersink a pilot hole near each corner of the front of the drawer box from the inside. With the drawer in place, position the face and clamp it so it doesn't move.

STEP 15: Drill pilot holes into the drawer face from inside the drawer, taking care not to drill all the way through. Drive screws into the top holes and then test the fit. If it's balanced in the opening, drive the other two screws.

STEP 16: Sand the base and drawer, working up to 180-grit, and then apply a finish of your choice.

STEP 17: Place the top upside down on a protected surface. Center the base, and then attach it to the top using screws driven through the side strechers.

Make a slight chamfer around the edges of the drawer face using a block plane.

Drawer Face Styles

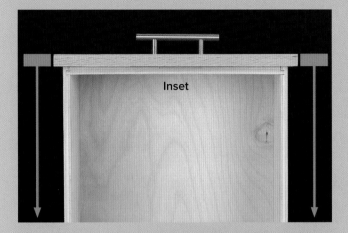

Inset drawer faces fit fully inside the face frame or frameless cabinet opening with the front surfaces flush. Inset drawer faces are the trickiest type to install because they must fit perfectly inside the face frame or the uneven gap (called the reveal) around the face will show the error.

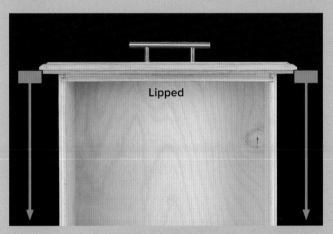

Lipped drawer faces have rabbets cut along the back edges to create a recess that fits over the face frame. The net effect is that the front surface of the drawer front will be ⅜" proud of the cabinet. Lipped drawers are not traditionally attached to a separate drawer box, but they can be.

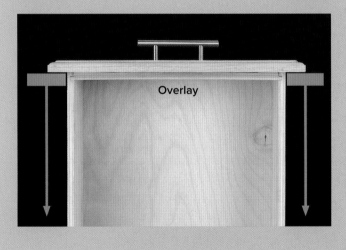

Overlay drawer faces close against the face frame. The front edges of the drawer front normally are profiled. Overlay drawer faces are the most common type used today because they are the easiest to make and install. Overlay faces are almost always used on frameless cabinets.

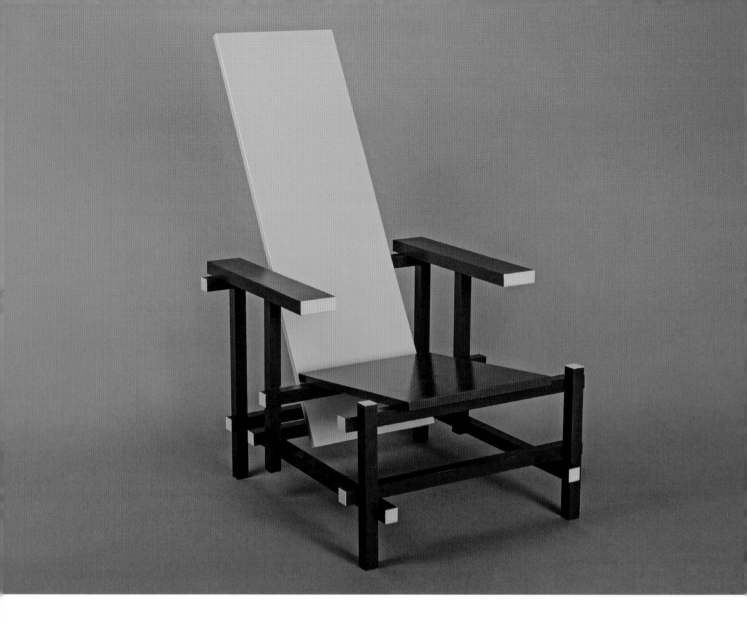

Rietveld Chair

A sturdy, buildable reproduction of a furniture-design icon.

This iconic chair was originally designed by Gerrit Rietveld in 1917. It's appealing to me because it's boiled down to the bare essentials, making it supereasy to build. Designed with the idea of mass production, Rietveld used common dimension lumber for the framework. At the time, that dimension was 1⅛", so everything but the seat and back are 1⅛" thick. In the spirit of common dimension lumber, you could alter this to 1½"—the standard thickness of 2× lumber. I kept the original dimensions, as I felt it looked a little heavy at 1½".

The chair I built is painted (rather painstakingly but worth the effort) like the original, with three contrasting colors. If you're not into the color scheme, take heart—the original design called for unstained beech. It wasn't until the early 1920s that Rietveld opted for painting it with primary colors. I used poplar to build my chair; it's strong, readily available, easy to work with, and takes paint well. To keep construction simple, I assembled the chair using only glue and screws at the joints. I added one part to the design for ease of construction and rigidity. If you can't figure out which part, then I've done my job!

RIETVELD CHAIR SHOPPING LIST

▶ Sandpaper (120-, 180-, 220-grit)
▶ Paint (enamel)

The arms and the chair undercarriage are made from poplar; an inexpensive but very durable hardwood sold at most building centers. All of the undercarriage parts are cut to the same 1⅛" x 1⅛" dimension; the arms are cut from wider, thicker stock. The seat and back are made from ½"-thick Baltic birch plywood, which has no voids and takes paint very well.

Trim-head wood screws have small heads, making them easy to conceal with wood putty or joint compound so they disappear once paint is applied.

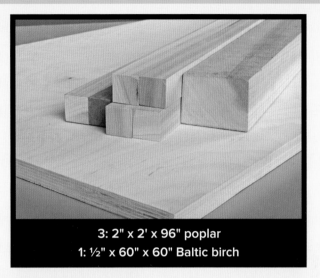

3: 2" x 2' x 96" poplar
1: ½" x 60" x 60" Baltic birch

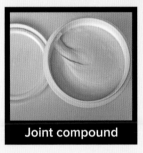

Joint compound

2" stainless steel trim-head screws

Wood glue

RIETVELD CHAIR CUT LIST

Overall Dimensions: 34" H × 33" D × 23 ¾" W

KEY	QTY	PART NAME	DIMENSION	MATERIAL
A	2	Front Frame Post	1⅛" × 1⅛" × 13"	Poplar
B	2	Middle Frame Post	1⅛" × 1⅛" × 15¹¹⁄₁₆"	Poplar
C	2	Back Frame Post	1⅛" × 1⅛" × 18½"	Poplar
D	5	Standard Cross Member	1⅛" × 1⅛" × 23¾"	Poplar
E	1	Upper Cross Member	1⅛" × 1⅛" × 26"	Poplar
F	2	Stretcher	1⅛" × 1⅛" × 26"	Poplar
G	2	Armrest	1⅛" × 3½" × 17¾"	Poplar
H	1	Seat	½" × 14" × 17¾"	Baltic Birch
I	1	Back	½" × 13" × 39¼"	Baltic Birch

How to Build a Rietveld Chair

STEP 1: The part preparation for this chair is greatly simplified by the fact that most of the parts are the same width and thickness (1⅛ × 1⅛"). You'll need to cut roughly 24 lineal feet of stock to this dimension (it's a good idea to cut some extra while you are set up, though). A table saw is perfect for this of course. You can also use a circular saw and straightedge guide, although the relatively small dimensions can get tricky to cut this way, so use extra caution. After cutting your stock to width and thickness, cut all the parts A through F to the listed length.

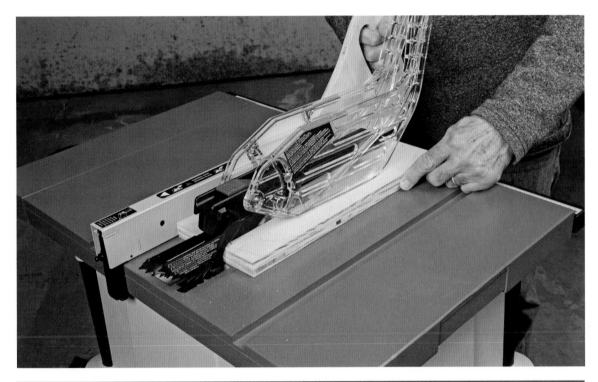

TIP: The smaller the parts you are cutting, generally speaking, the more dangerous the cutting becomes. If you are using a table saw to rip-cut thin strips of stock, be sure to use a sturdy push stick and to make sure the blade guard is in place and the riving knife at the outfeed end is positioned correctly (the riving knife fits into the saw kerf as you cut, preventing it from closing up or binding).

STEP 2: Cut the armrests to width and thickness from 2 × 4 stock. If your stock has rounded "bullnose" edges trim them off, even though this will mean that the armrest width is slightly under the listed 3½". Also cut the arms to length. One of the great features of this design is that all the parts are square-cut: no angle-cutting required.

STEP 3: Lay out and drill ³⁄₃₂"-diameter clearance holes for the screws that attach the frame parts together. Because the stock is relatively thin, use only one trimhead screw (and an even coat of glue) at each joint. Make a guide to help ensure that the screw locations are uniform at the joints (see tip). Because you will be driving 2" screws into two parts that are a combined 2¼" thickness, take care not to drive the screws too far.

TIP: Make a drilling guide to predrill clearance holes for all the cross members, as their locations should be uniform and centered. Use a plywood scrap to make the guide base and tack thin wood registration guides to one side and one end. The ³⁄₃₂" guide hole in the drilling guide should be centered edge to edge, ⁹⁄₁₆" from each edge and 1¾" from the end.

9⁄16"

1¾"

Drilling guide

FEATURED TIP

Spacer Blocks

To assemble this chair, it's helpful to make spacer blocks from scrap plywood to accurately position all the parts during assembly. The blocks not only establish the position of the parts, they help pin the parts in place during assembly. In the front assembly seen below, a 5"-long block is being used to register the bottom stretcher. The same block may be used to set the position for the bottom stretcher on the back assembly.

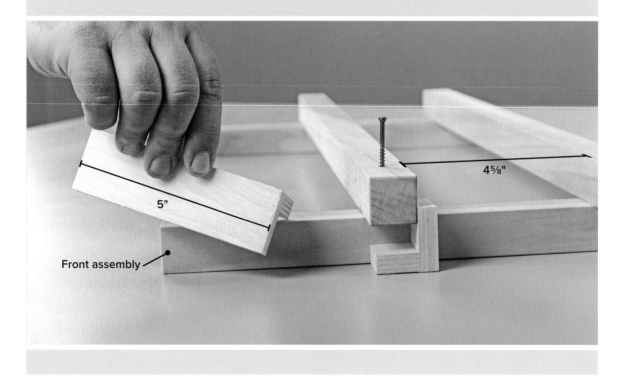

4⁵⁄₈"

5"

Front assembly

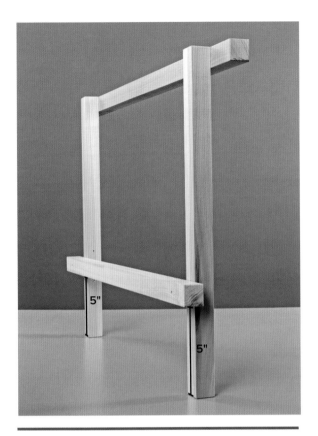

BACK SUBFRAME ASSEMBLY
upports the seat back.

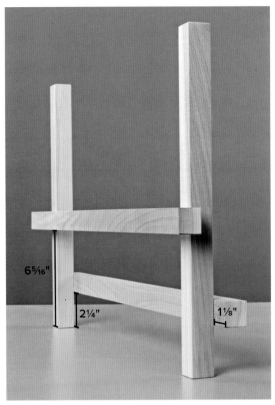

MIDDLE SUBFRAME ASSEMBLY provides most
of the bearing support for the seat.

STEP 4: Assemble the chair frame in three sections,
or *subframes*: the front frame, middle frame, and back
frame. Apply wood glue and drive one 2" trim-head
wood screw at each joint. Use a try square or framing
square to test and make sure the joined members fit
together at exactly 90° angles.

STEP 5: Finish the frame by attaching the subframes to
the long stretchers with glue and one trim-head screw
per joint. Test that the joint angles are perpendicular.
Once the chair frame is fully assembled and square,
add the armrests.

FRONT SUBFRAME ASSEMBLY stabilizes the chair
front and provides bearing for the seat board.

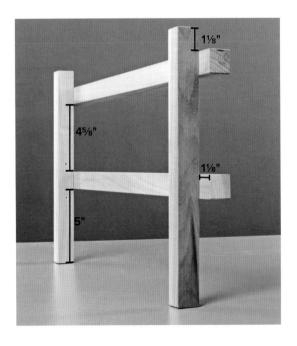

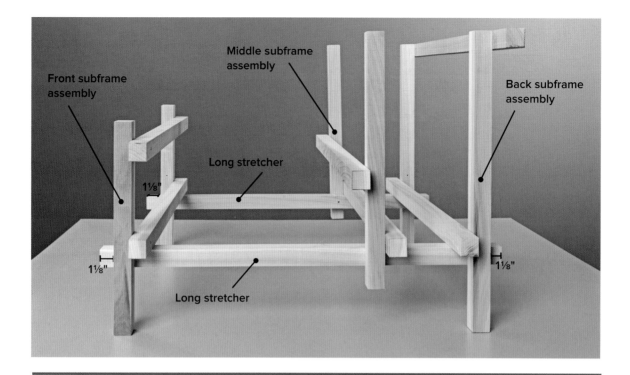

SET BASE ASSEMBLY is created by joining the three subframe assemblies with the long stretchers. Once the assembly is square you can add the armrests and then the seat and back.

STEP 6: Cut the seat board and backrest board to size from no-void plywood and then sand them smooth. Set them in place and mark the points where the screws should be driven to attach them to the horizontal members in the seat base subframes. Drill clearance holes for these screws. NOTE: For strength and ease of construction, all of the joints in the seat base are 90° joints. Because the seat and back are both angled, this necessarily means that the broad plywood parts will not be perfectly flush against the base parts that support them. Don't worry about it. This does not have a negative impact on the bearing ability of the seat base. Use three or four 1½" trim-head screws at each bearing point, drilling the clearance holes so they are perpendicular to the face of the seat and back rest.

STEP 7: Fill all the screw head holes in the frame with wood putty or spackle, and then sand the dried putty so it is smooth with the surrounding wood surface. Ease any sharp corners on the frame parts by sanding or with a small block plane. Don't go overboard—you want to retain the visual geometry of all the square parts and joints.

STEP 8: Apply a finish of your choice to the frame, seat, and back before assembling them. If you are using a traditional red-and-blue paint scheme (see page 153) or another contrasting paint scheme like the one I used, the painting of parts will make or break the success of your project. Take your time to make sure you get crisp lines where colors meet and smooth, brushstroke-free surfaces. The best way to accomplish this is to paint on primer first and then apply at least two or three thin coats of paint to each part.

STEP 9: Fasten the seat and back to the frame using 2" trim-head screws. Make sure to drill pilot holes into the frame cross members before driving the screws. Fill the screw holes using spackling compound and touch up the paint to cover the screw heads.

The *Red and Blue Chair* designed by Gerrit Reitveld in 1917 is one of the most iconic chairs in the history of design. Versions of it are displayed in the permanent collections of several museums, including the Metropolitan Museum of Modern Art in New York City. The chair project seen here is an interpretation of the *Reitveld Chair*, with only one structural part added. The color scheme in the finished project diverges from the original *Red and Blue*, of course, but color mavens out there will note that the paints chosen are all secondary colors from the original tones.

Floating Shelf

Despite its gravity-defying appearance, this shelf is plenty sturdy.

While this shelf appears to be floating on the wall, it's strong enough to support a serious collection of books or other weighty curiosities. The shelf gets its strength from two things: First, all of the sections are "torsion boxes," meaning they are constructed with an inner web frame that's covered by a thin skin of ¼"-thick plywood, in much the same way that hollow-core partition doors are manufactured. This not only makes for a rigid shelf, but it also results in parts that are much lighter than if they were cut from solid wood. Second, the shelves are attached to wall cleats, which are firmly secured to wall studs. Cover the boxes with an adhesive-backed veneer of your favorite wood species—they will look like solid slabs of wood, but without all the weight.

FLOATING SHELF SHOPPING LIST

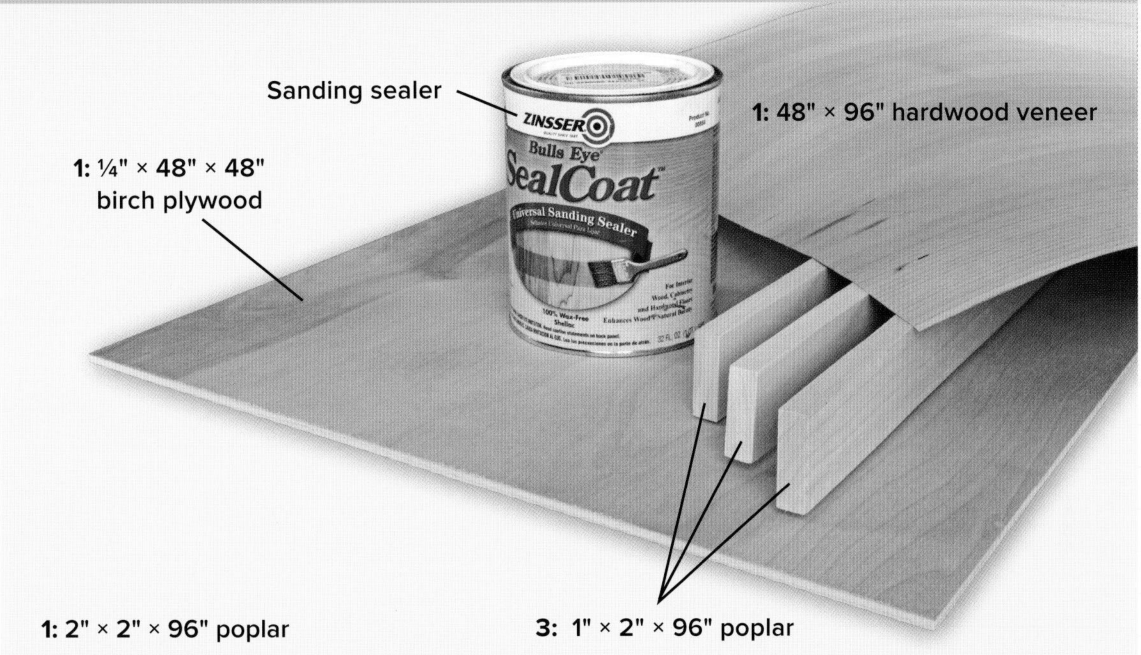

Sanding sealer
1: 48" × 96" hardwood veneer
1: ¼" × 48" × 48"
birch plywood
ZINSSER
Bulls Eye
SealCoat
Universal Sanding Sealer
1: 2" × 2" × 96" poplar
3: 1" × 2" × 96" poplar

▶ wood finish

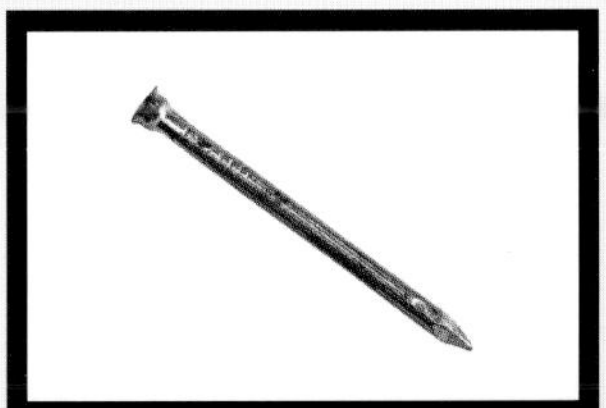

Finish nails

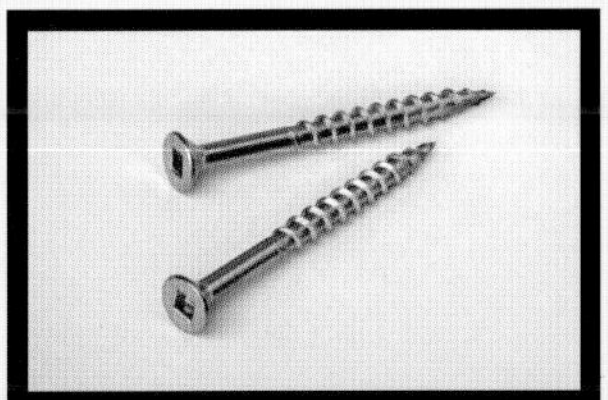

Wood screws

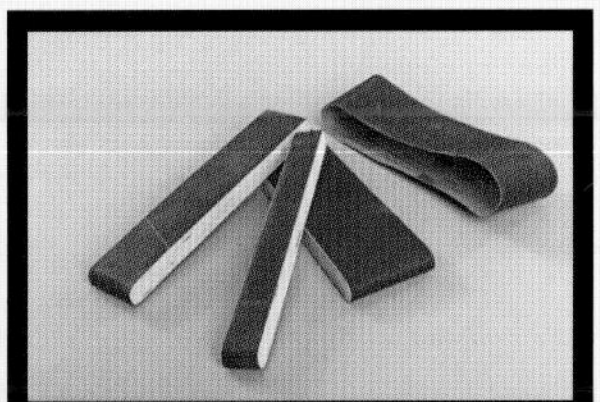

Sanding belts

*POPLAR: I used thin, narrow strips of poplar to make the webbing for the insides of these torsion boxes. Poplar is easy to find and work with. Its strength and hardness are pluses for the project, but perhaps the best quality it has is dimensional stability. It holds its shape and dimensions better than most woods when temperature and humidity change. A less stable webbing wood, such as pine, is more likely to open gaps in the boxes and veneer as the environmental conditions change in your room.

FLOATING SHELF CUT LIST

Overall Dimensions: 12 H × 10" D × 36½" W

KEY	QTY	PART NAME	DIMENSION	MATERIAL
A	4	Shelf Frame Ends	½" × 1½" × 9½"	Poplar
B	4	Shelf Frame Centers	½" × 1½" × 7¼"	Poplar
C	1	Long Shelf Front	½" × 1½" × 22½"	Poplar
D	1	Long Shelf Back	½" × 1½" × 21½"	Poplar
E	1	Short Shelf Front	½" × 1½" × 12"	Poplar
F	1	Short Shelf Back	½" × 1½" × 11"	Poplar
G	2	Vertical Ends	1½" × 2" × 10"	Poplar
H	1	Vertical Center	½ × 1½" × 9"	Poplar
I	2	Vertical Front & Back	½ × 1½" × 8"	Poplar
J	2	Long Shelf Skin	¼" × 10" × 22½"	Birch Plywood
K	2	Short Shelf Skin	¼" × 10" × 12"	Birch Plywood
L	2	Vertical Skin	¼" × 10" × 12"	Birch Plywood

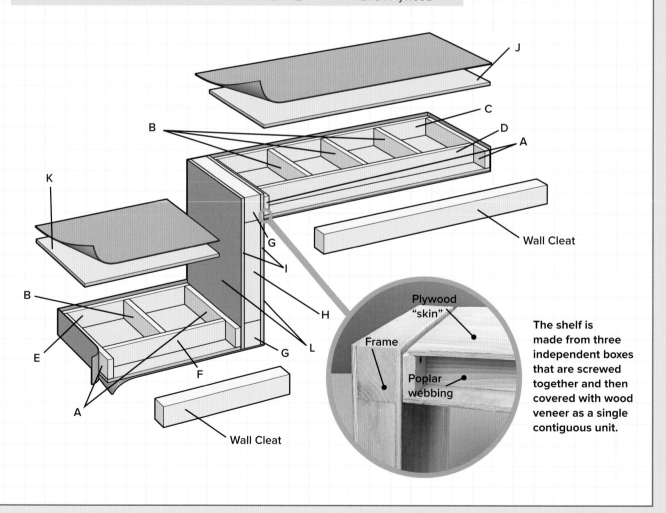

Wall Cleat

Wall Cleat

Plywood "skin"

Frame

Poplar webbing

The shelf is made from three independent boxes that are screwed together and then covered with wood veneer as a single contiguous unit.

How to Build a Floating Shelf

STEP 1: Mill all of your poplar stock to ½" thickness. Except for two 10"-long pieces, all the ½" stock should be cut to 1½" width. Cut the inner slats to length to begin creating the webbing. Then, assemble the three individual frames using glue and finish nails.

STEP 2: Cut the plywood panels ("skins") to fit both faces of the vertical shelf section. Apply the plywood panels to both sides of the vertical, using glue and finish nails. Apply only the bottom panels to the horizontal frames. All these panels should be flush with the webbing frame on all sides.

STEP 3: Sand the edges of each section so the panel edges are flush with the frames. Cover both faces of the vertical section with self-adhesive wood veneer (see page 112 for details on applying veneer). TIP: To improve the bond between the plywood skins and the wood veneer, apply a thin coat of sanding sealer onto the plywood surfaces and let it dry before you apply the pressure-sensitive veneer.

STEP 4: Drive three or four wood screws through the end framing members that mate against the top and bottom of the vertical box. Apply glue at the joint first. The open top of the top shelf box should be the thickness of the plywood panel below the top of the vertical box. The bottom, plywood-clad surface of the bottom shelf should be flush with the bottom of the vertical box.

The open faces of the top and the bottom horizontal shelf boxes should be oriented upward when the boxes are joined together.

STEP 5: Cut the top plywood skin for each horizontal box so the veneer also covers the top and bottom of the vertical box. Attach the top panels to the two shelves using glue and finish nails. Sand the edges of these panels flush with the frames.

STEP 6: Apply self-adhesive wood veneer to the remaining shelf surfaces. For best visual appearance, the sequence you use to install the veneer pieces is very important. You want as few visible seams as possible. To accomplish this, install the veneer in the following order: outer ends, bottom surfaces, vertical edge, horizontal edges, top surfaces.

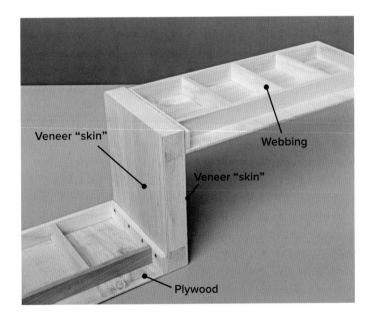

Veneer "skin"

Webbing

Veneer "skin"

Plywood

After applying each piece of veneer, trim the excess with a sharp utility knife or craft knife and sand flush before applying the next piece.

STEP 7: Sand the whole surface and apply a finish of your choice. Veneer is already sanded from the factory, so you can go straight to 220-grit.

FEATURED SKILL

Scribing to a Wall

Before fastening the shelf to the wall cleats, have a helper hold it in place. Scribe all the way around the shelf. Use a belt sander to sand to the lines so your shelf will perfectly match the contour of the wall.

Place a pencil flat on the wall, held vertically. Slide it along the wall with the point on the shelf, allowing it to mark any variance in the wall onto the shelf.

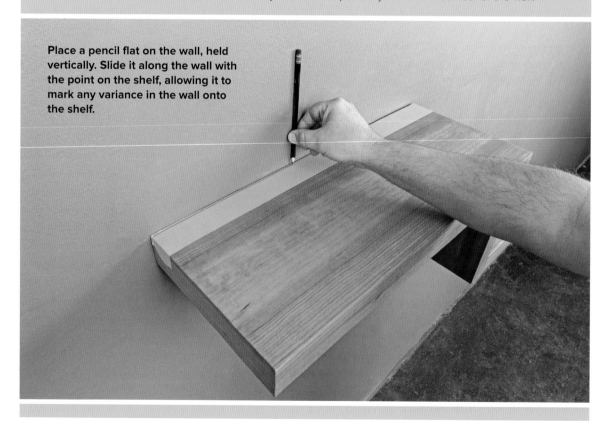

Hanging Torsion Box Shelves

The two horizontal shelf sections have a recess in their back edges. Cut a wall cleat to fit each recess. Make the cleats ¼" shallower than the full depth of the recess. For example, these shelves have a 1¾"-deep recess, so make the wall cleats 1½" deep. This allows room to scribe the shelves to the wall if needed. Secure the long cleat to the wall studs, and then slide the shelf onto it. With the shelf in position, mark the position of the other horizontal section. Install a cleat for this section as well.

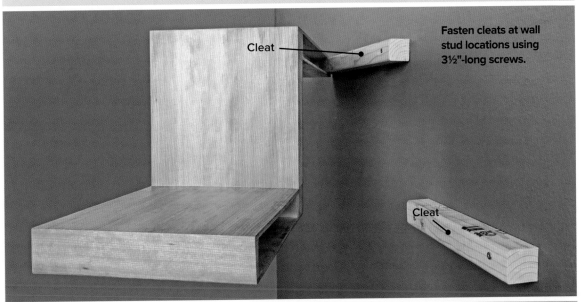

Cleat

Fasten cleats at wall stud locations using 3½"-long screws.

Cleat

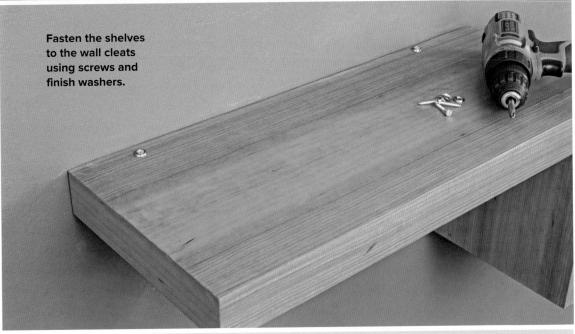

Fasten the shelves to the wall cleats using screws and finish washers.

Danish Modern Buffet

A sleek, efficient and surprisingly buildable example of the retro-popular Danish Modern style.

This piece brings me back to my childhood. It's similar to my parents' record player cabinet, sliding doors and all. All the albums were stored inside; kid stuff on one side and grown-up stuff on the other. With the resurgence of vinyl, this might be just the place to set up your hi-fi system. With the addition of shelves, it is also perfect storage for tablecloths, napkins, placemats, and seldom-used dinnerware. The big difference between this cabinet and the one I remember from my youth is the construction; the old one was poorly made and didn't have a skirt between the legs, so it sagged a bit under the weight of all the vinyl. This new iteration is well-made, and with a wise economy of design that keeps it from being bulky and heavy. Plus, it has the design charm that is behind the resurgence in popularity of the Danish Modern style.

DANISH MODERN BUFFET SHOPPING LIST

1: 1" × 4" × 96" solid cherry

1: ¾" × 48" × 96" cherry plywood

1: ¼" × 48" × 48" cherry plywood

1: 2" × 2" × 48" solid cherry

▶ Shelf supports
▶ Biscuits
▶ Finishing materials
▶ ⅜" dowels
▶ Masking tape
▶ Solid wood edge banding
▶ Wood glue
▶ Ebony stain
▶ Danish oil

Finish nails

Sandpaper
(120-, 180-grit)

DANISH MODERN BUFFET CUT LIST

Overall Dimensions: 27" H × 20" D × 47" W

KEY	QTY	PART NAME	DIMENSION	MATERIAL
A	2	Top & Bottom Panel	¾" × 18" × 46"	Cherry Plywood
B	2	End Panel	¾" × 18¼" × 19¼"	Cherry Plywood
C	1	Center Panel	¾" × 16⅝" × 19¼"	Cherry Plywood
D	2	Shelf	¾" × 16" × 22⅛"	Cherry Plywood
E	2	Top & Bottom Front Edging	¾" × 2" × 47"	Cherry
F	2	Top & Bottom End Edging	¾" × ½" × 18"	Cherry
G	3	Vertical Edgebanding	¼" × ¾" × 19¼"	Cherry
H	1	Back	¼" × 20" × 45⅞"	Cherry Plywood
I	4	Leg	2" × 2" × 6¼"	Cherry
J	2	Front & Back Skirt	¾" × 2¼" × 38¼"	Cherry Plywood
K	2	End Skirt	¾" × 2¼" × 10¼"	Cherry Plywood
L	2	Door	¼" × 19½" × 23"	Cherry Plywood

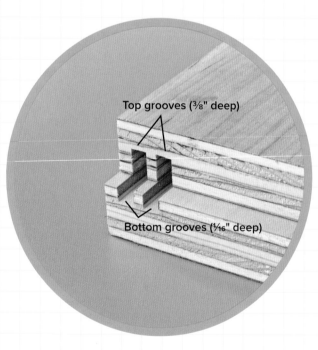

Top grooves (⅜" deep)

Bottom grooves (¹⁄₁₆" deep)

Sliding door groove detail. The grooves for the sliding doors should be about ¹⁄₃₂" wider than the door material's thickness. The top grooves are deeper than the bottom grooves to allow door installation after assembly.

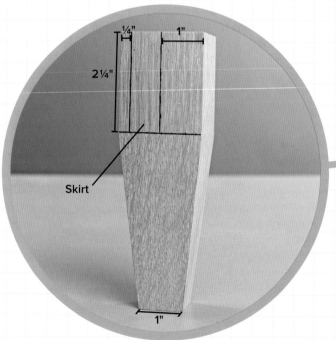

¼" 1"

2¼"

Skirt

1"

Tapered leg detail

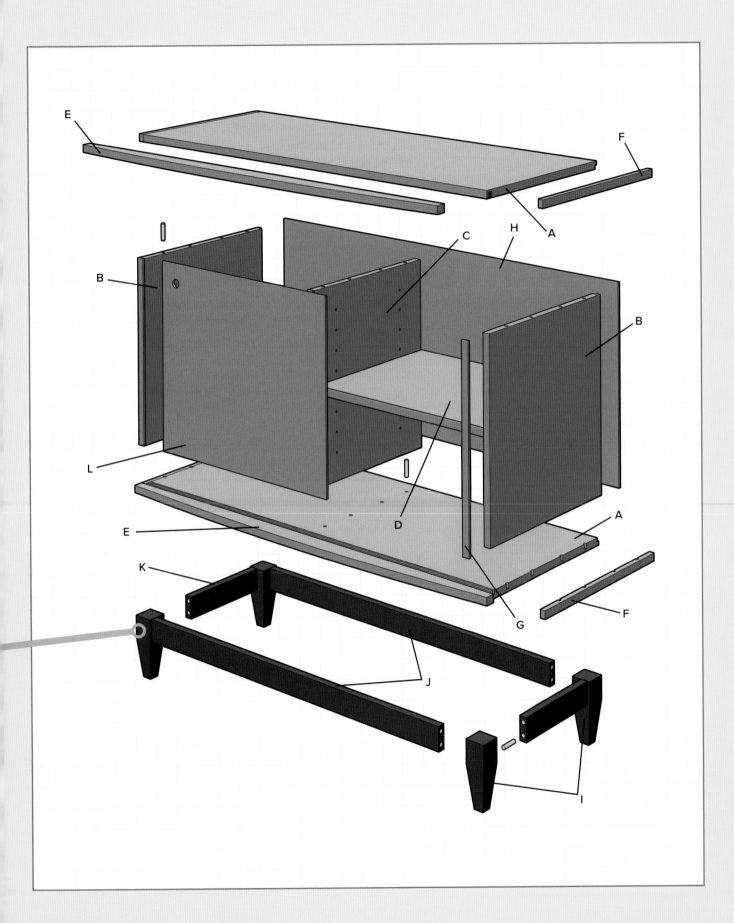

How to Build a Danish Modern Buffet

STEP 1: Cut the top, bottom, and side panels to size from ¾"-thick plywood. Use a cabinet-grade plywood for this project. I chose cherry plywood, but others with a smooth, clear surface—such as walnut or birch or maple—will also work. Just make sure you choose solid wood stock that matches. Also make sure the species you choose is available in ¼"-thick sheet stock as well.

STEP 2: Cut the door grooves in the top and bottom, using a table saw or a circular saw and straightedge cutting guide. This will take at least two passes for each groove, depending on the thickness of your doors and your blade's kerf.

STEP 3: Cut the rabbets to house the back panel on the back edges of the top, bottom, and side panels. Use a router or table saw to make the rabbet cuts.

STEP 4: Mill the ¼"-thick by ¾" wide solid wood edging for the front edges of the side plywood panels to width, depth, and rough length. Also mill the stock for the side edging pieces on the top and bottom panels, which should be ½" thick by ¾" wide. The solid wood edging for the front edges of the top and bottom panels is milled to ¾" thick by 2" wide so it can be trimmed later with an arc shape.

STEP 5: Apply edging to the front edges of the cabinet sides and center vertical using glue and clamps. When the glue is dry, sand the edging flush with the plywood surfaces.

STEP 6: Apply the 2"-wide front edging to the top and bottom panels using glue, clamps, and biscuits for alignment. Note that these edging strips should cover the end grain of the side edging strips. Apply the side edging first, followed by the front edging strip. TIP: Use biscuits (see page 140) to help with the alignment of the wider front edging strips. When the glue is dry, sand the faces to make sure the edging is flush with the plywood.

STEP 7: Cut the arcs on the front edges of the top and bottom panels with a jigsaw or band saw. Even out the curves with a sanding block.

Use a slat and string (see page 101) to lay out the top and bottom front-edge arcs after the solid wood edging strips are attached. Cut off the waste just outside of the cutting lines and smooth out the arcs.

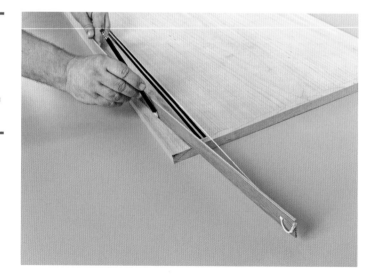

STEP 8: Drill dowel holes into the end

QUICK TIP

Shelf Support Drilling Guide

Cut a 1½" × 1½" × 18" piece of hardwood. Drill a ¼"-diameter hole using a drill press, every 2" on center. Clearly mark which end you'll use as the bottom reference.

To use the guide, clamp it against the cabinet side and drill ¼"-diameter holes using a depth stop.

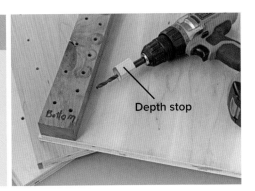

Depth stop

panels and center panel, and then use dowel centers to locate the mating holes on the top and bottom panels (see page 38). Drill these holes using a depth stop (see page 68).

STEP 9: Drill holes for the shelf supports in the center divider and the end panels (see above). This is much easier to do before the cabinet is assembled.

STEP 10: Assemble the cabinet using glue and clamps. Make sure you check the corners with a square.

STEP 11: Cut the back panel, and fasten it into the rabbet in the backs of the tops, sides, and bottom panels using glue and finish nails.

STEP 12: Cut the base skirt pieces and the blanks for the legs (see page 163). I used ¾" cherry plywood for the skirt boards because it does not have wood movement issues, but you can use hardwood if you'd rather. Lay out and drill holes for the dowel joints in the base parts.

STEP 13: Cut the leg stock to size: a full 2" x 2". Taper the legs (see page 167), sand all the base parts, and assemble the base using glue and clamps.

Attach the skirt pieces to the flat area on the legs using dowels to make a strong, durable joint.

STEP 14: Apply ebony stain to the base and allow it to dry overnight.

STEP 15: Drill clearance (pilot) holes with counterbores into the skirt boards. Attach the base to the cabinet using glue and screws.

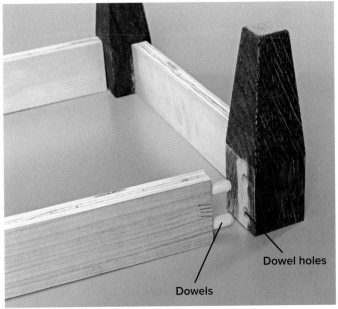

Dowel holes

Dowels

Applying Solid Wood Edgebanding

Solid wood edgebanding is used to cover the edge of plywood or other sheet stock. Apply glue to the plywood and then work the edgebanding back and forth on the glued edge until it starts to stick. Clamp the edgebanding in place using a clamping caul. For longer pieces, I typically attach the banding with a pin nailer prior to clamping, just to hold it in place.

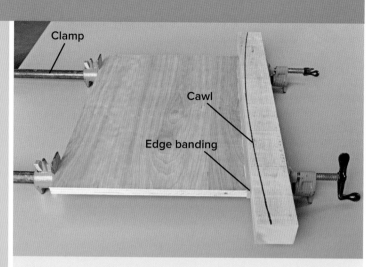

Clamp

Cawl

Edge banding

Make edgebanding no more than 1/16" wider than the edge it will cover. Use a clamping caul to spread the clamps' pressure over the whole piece. A clamping caul is just a thick board that has a slight curve. The convex side of the curve faces the part you're clamping. You can usually find ready-made clamping cauls in the pile of 2 × 4s at the home center.

Use a depth stop when you drill the counterbores to make sure that your screws sink to the right depth and won't poke through the inside of the cabinet.

Depth stop

STEP 16: Cut the doors and then drill their finger holes. Use a sacrificial backer board when you drill these to prevent blowout on the back side.

STEP 17: Tape around the finger holes and carefully paint their inside edges black.

STEP 18: Sand the cabinet and doors, working your way up to 180-grit, and then apply a finish of your choice. After the finish is dry, slip the doors into place by tilting them and inserting the top all the way into its slot, so you can fit the door in the cabinet, and then lower it into the bottom slot.

I applied three coats of Danish oil finish to this piece. It leaves a soft luster and no brush marks. To apply, wipe on a generous amount, allowing it to soak in for about 15 minutes. Wipe off any excess and allow it to dry overnight before applying the next coat. Between the second and third coats, sand the surface lightly using 600-grit wet-or-dry paper using some Danish oil as a lubricant. If the top surface will see heavy use, apply a topcoat of polyurethane for extra protection.

FEATURED SKILL

Tapering Short Legs

To make shallow tapers, you'll need a tapering jig for your tablesaw. You can easily make your own as shown on page 120. The legs on this buffet are too short for tapering individually, so start with a blank that's at least 12" long.

Lay out a leg at each end of the blank and cut the tapers. After tapering, cut the legs free of the blank.

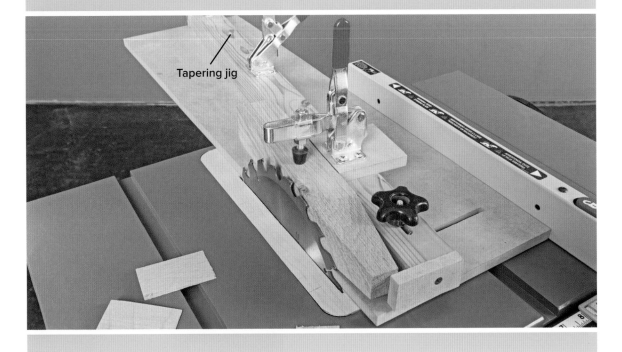

Tapering jig

APPENDIX A: NAILS

The wide variety of nail styles and sizes makes it possible to choose exactly the right fastener for each job. Nails are identified by their typical purpose, such as casing, flooring, or roofing nails; or by a physical feature, such as galvanized, coated, or spiral. Some nails come in both a galvanized and non-galvanized version. Use galvanized nails for outdoor projects and non-galvanized indoors. Nail lengths may be specified in inches or by numbers from 4 to 60 followed by the letter "d," which stands for "penny" (see "Nail Sizes," opposite page).

Some of the most popular nails for carpentry projects include:

- Common and box nails for general framing work. Box nails are smaller in diameter, which makes them less likely to split wood. Box nails were designed for constructing boxes and crates, but they can be used in any application where thin, dry wood will be nailed close to the edge of the piece. Most common and box nails have a cement or vinyl coating that improves their holding power.
- Finish and casing nails, which have small heads and are driven just below the work surface with a nail set. Finish nails are used for attaching moldings and other trim to walls. Casing nails are used for nailing window and door casings. They have a slightly larger head than finish nails for better holding power.
- Brads, small wire nails sometimes referred to as finish nails. They are used primarily in cabinetry, where very small nail holes are preferred.
- Flooring nails, which are often spiral-shanked for extra holding power to prevent floorboards from separating or squeaking. Spiral flooring nails are sometimes used in other applications, such as installing tongue-and-groove paneling on ceilings.
- Galvanized nails, which have a zinc coating that resists rusting. They are used for outdoor projects.
- Wallboard nails, once the standard fastener for wallboard, are less common today because of the development of Phillips-head wallboard screws that drive quickly with a screw gun or drill and offer superior holding power (page 170).

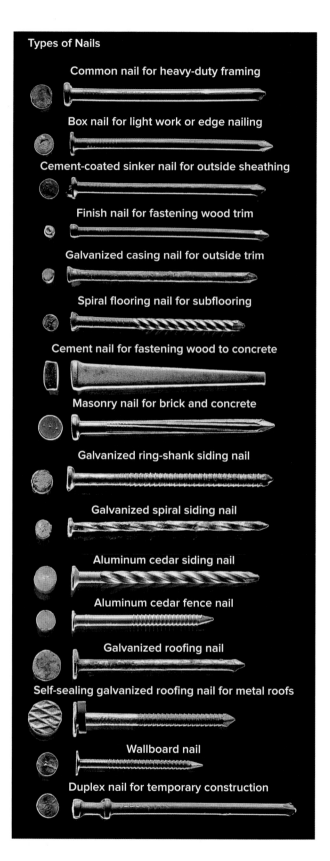

Types of Nails

Common nail for heavy-duty framing

Box nail for light work or edge nailing

Cement-coated sinker nail for outside sheathing

Finish nail for fastening wood trim

Galvanized casing nail for outside trim

Spiral flooring nail for subflooring

Cement nail for fastening wood to concrete

Masonry nail for brick and concrete

Galvanized ring-shank siding nail

Galvanized spiral siding nail

Aluminum cedar siding nail

Aluminum cedar fence nail

Galvanized roofing nail

Self-sealing galvanized roofing nail for metal roofs

Wallboard nail

Duplex nail for temporary construction

NAIL SIZES

The pennyweight scale that manufacturers use to size nails was developed centuries ago as an approximation of the number of pennies it would take to buy 100 nails of that size. The range of nail types available today (and what they cost) is much wider, but the scale is still in use. Each pennyweight refers to a specific length (see chart, below), although you will find slight variations in length from one nail type to the next. For example, box nails of a given pennyweight are roughly ⅛" shorter than common nails of the same weight.

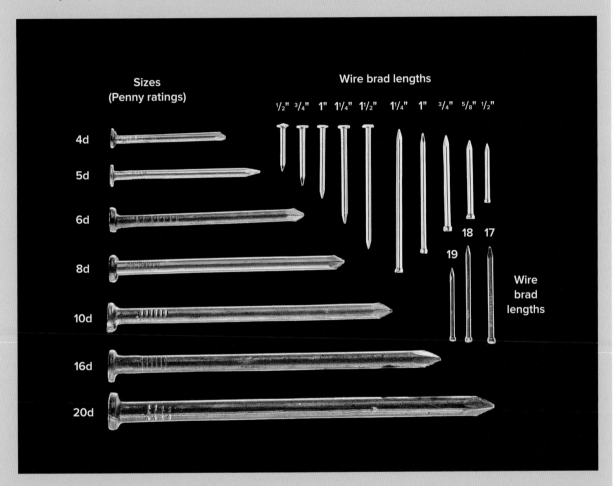

Estimating Nail Quantities

Estimate the number of nails you'll need for a project, then use the chart to determine approximately how many pounds of nails to purchase.

Note: *Sizes and quantities not listed are less common, although they may be available through some manufacturers.*

Nails per lb.

Pennyweight	2d	3d	4d	5d	6d	7d	8d	10d	12d	16d	20d
Length (in.)	1	1¼	1½	1⅝	2	2⅛	2½	3	3¼	3½	4
Common	870	543	294	254	167		101	66	61	47	29
Box	635	473	406	236	210	145	94	88	71	39	
Cement-coated			527	387	293	223	153	111	81	64	52
Finish	1350	880	630	535	288		196	124	113	93	39
Masonry			155	138	100	78	64	48	43	34	

APPENDIX B: SCREWS & OTHER HARDWARE

The advent of the screw gun and numerous types of driver bits for drills have made screws a mainstay of the carpentry trade. With literally hundreds of different screws and types of fastening hardware available, there is a specific screw for almost every job. But, for most carpentry jobs you will only need to consider a few general-purpose types. Although nails are still preferred for framing jobs, screws have replaced nails for hanging wallboard, installing blocking between studs, and attaching sheathing and flooring. Screws are also used to attach a workpiece to plaster, brick, or concrete, which requires an anchoring device.

Screws are categorized according to length, slot style, head shape, and gauge. The thickness of the screw body is indicated by the gauge number. The larger the number, the larger the screw. Large screws provide extra holding power; small screws are less likely to split a workpiece. There are various styles of screw slot, including Phillips, slotted, and square. Square-drive screwdrivers are increasing in popularity because they grip the screw head tightly, but Phillips head screws are still the most popular.

Twist anchor screw · Galvanized deck screw · Lag screw

Round-head wood screw · Pan-head sheet-metal screw · Flat-head wood screw

Hi-low screw · Flat-head Phillips wood screw · Wallboard screw · Hex-head sheet-metal screw

WALLBOARD SCREWS & DECK SCREWS

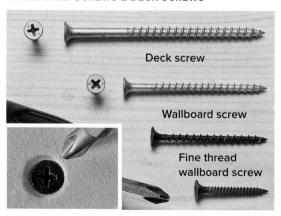

Deck screw

Wallboard screw

Fine thread wallboard screw

Use wallboard screws for general-purpose, convenient fastening. Easily recognizable by their bugle-shaped heads, wallboard screws are designed to dimple the surface of the wallboard without ripping the facing paper (inset). However, they are often used for non-wallboard projects because they drive easily with a drill or screw gun, don't require pilot holes, and seldom pop up as wood dries. In soft wood, the bugle-shaped heads allow the screws to countersink themselves. Deck screws are corrosion-resistant wallboard screws made specifically for outdoor use.

APPENDIX C: GLUES & ADHESIVES

When used properly, glues and adhesives can be stronger than the materials they hold together. Use hot glue in lightweight woodworking projects, carpenter's glue for wood joints, and carpentry adhesive for preliminary installation of thin panels and lumber. Panel adhesive, a thinner formula that can be applied from a tube or with a brush, is used to install paneling, wainscoting, and other lightweight tongue-and-groove materials. Most caulk is applied with a caulk gun, but some types are available in squeeze tubes for smaller applications. Caulks are designed to permanently close joints, fill gaps in woodwork, and hide subtle imperfections. Different caulks are made of different compounds and vary greatly in durability and workability. While silicone caulks last longer, they are not paintable and are difficult to smooth out. Latex caulks are less durable than silicone, but are much easier to work with, especially when used to hide gaps. Many caulks are rated on scales of 1 to 4 to indicate how well they bond to masonry, glass, tile, metals, wood, fiberglass, and plastic. Read the label carefully to choose the right caulk for the job.

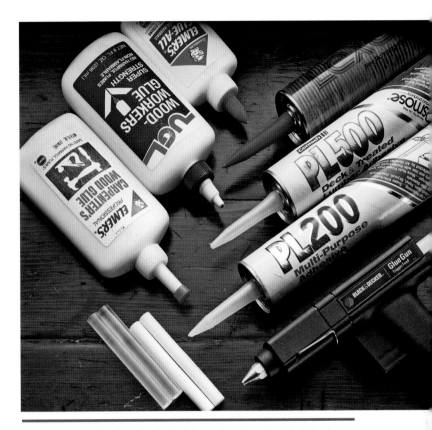

Carpentry adhesives include (clockwise from top right): clear adhesive caulk, for sealing gaps in damp areas; waterproof construction adhesive, for bonding lumber for outdoor projects; multi-purpose adhesive, for attaching paneling and forming strong bonds between lumber pieces; electric hot glue gun and glue sticks, for bonding small decorative trim pieces on built-ins; wood glues and all-purpose glue, for many woodworking projects.

APPENDIX D: METRIC CONVERSIONS

ENGLISH TO METRIC

TO CONVERT:	TO:	MULTIPLY BY:
Inches	Millimeters	25.4
Inches	Centimeters	2.54
Feet	Meters	0.305
Yards	Meters	0.914
Square inches	Square centimeters	6.45
Square feet	Square meters	0.093
Square yards	Square meters	0.836
Ounces	Milliliters	30.0
Pints (US)	Liters	0.473 (Imp. 0.568)
Quarts (US)	Liters	0.946 (Imp. 1.136)
Gallons (US)	Liters	3.785 (Imp. 4.546)
Ounces	Grams	28.4
Pounds	Kilograms	0.454

TO CONVERT:	TO:	MULTIPLY BY:
Millimeters	Inches	0.039
Centimeters	Inches	0.394
Meters	Feet	3.28
Meters	Yards	1.09
Square centimeters	Square inches	0.155
Square meters	Square feet	10.8
Square meters	Square yards	1.2
Milliliters	Ounces	.033
Liters	Pints (US)	2.114 (Imp. 1.76)
Liters	Quarts (US)	1.057 (Imp. 0.88)
Liters	Gallons (US)	0.264 (Imp. 0.22)
Grams	Ounces	0.035
Kilograms	Pounds	2.2

LUMBER DIMENSIONS

NOMINAL - U.S.	ACTUAL - U.S. (IN INCHES)	METRIC
1 × 2	¾ × 1½	19 × 38 mm
1 × 3	¾ × 2½	19 × 64 mm
1 × 4	¾ × 3½	19 × 89 mm
1 × 5	¾ × 4½	19 × 114 mm
1 × 6	¾ × 5½	19 × 140 mm
1 × 7	¾ × 6¼	19 × 159 mm
1 × 8	¾ × 7¼	19 × 184 mm
1 × 10	¾ × 9¼	19 × 235 mm
1 × 12	¾ × 11¼	19 × 286 mm
1¼ × 4	1 × 3½	25 × 89 mm
1¼ × 6	1 × 5½	25 × 140 mm
1¼ × 8	1 × 7¼	25 × 184 mm
1¼ × 10	1 × 9¼	25 × 235 mm
1¼ × 12	1 × 11¼	25 × 286 mm
1½ × 4	1¼ × 3½	32 × 89 mm
1½ × 6	1¼ × 5½	32 × 140 mm
1½ × 8	1¼ × 7¼	32 × 184 mm
1½ × 10	1¼ × 9¼	32 × 235 mm
1½ × 12	1¼ × 11¼	32 × 286 mm
2 × 4	1½ × 3½	38 × 89 mm
2 × 6	1½ × 5½	38 × 140 mm
2 × 8	1½ × 7¼	38 × 184 mm
2 × 10	1½ × 9¼	38 × 235 mm
2 × 12	1½ × 11¼	38 × 286 mm
3 × 6	2½ × 5½	64 × 140 mm
4 × 4	3½ × 3½	89 × 89 mm
4 × 6	3½ × 5½	89 × 140 mm

CONVERTING TEMPERATURES

Convert degrees Fahrenheit (F) to degrees Celsius (C) by following this simple formula: Subtract 32 from the Fahrenheit temperature reading. Then multiply that number by $\frac{5}{9}$. For example, 77°F - 32 = 45. 45 × $\frac{5}{9}$ = 25°C.

To convert degrees Celsius to degrees Fahrenheit, multiply the Celsius temperature reading by $\frac{9}{5}$. Then, add 32. For example, 25°C × $\frac{9}{5}$ = 45. 45 + 32 = 77°F.

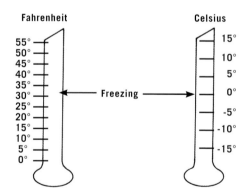

LIQUID MEASUREMENT EQUIVALENTS

1 Pint	= 16 Fluid Ounces	= 2 Cups
1 Quart	= 32 Fluid Ounces	= 2 Pints
1 Gallon	= 128 Fluid Ounces	= 4 Quarts

METRIC PLYWOOD PANELS

Metric plywood panels are commonly available in two sizes: 1,200 mm × 2,400 mm and 1,220 mm × 2,400 mm, which is roughly equivalent to a 4 × 8' sheet. Standard and Select sheathing panels come in standard thicknesses, while Sanded grade panels are available in special thicknesses.

STANDARD SHEATHING GRADE		SANDED GRADE	
7.5 mm	(⁵⁄₁₆")	6 mm	(⁴⁄₁₇")
9.5 mm	(³⁄₈")	8 mm	(⁵⁄₁₆")
12.5 mm	(½")	11 mm	(⁷⁄₁₆")
15.5 mm	(⁵⁄₈")	14 mm	(⁹⁄₁₆")
18.5 mm	(¾")	17 mm	(²⁄₃ ")
20.5 mm	(¹³⁄₁₆")	19 mm	(¾")
22.5 mm	(⅞")	21 mm	(¹³⁄₁₆")
25.5 mm	(1")	24 mm	(¹⁵⁄₁₆")

COUNTERBORE, SHANK & PILOT HOLE DIAMETERS

SCREW SIZE	COUNTERBORE DIAMETER FOR SCREW HEAD (IN INCHES)	CLEARANCE HOLE FOR SCREW SHANK (IN INCHES)	PILOT HOLE DIAMETER	
			HARD WOOD (IN INCHES)	SOFT WOOD (IN INCHES)
#1	.146 (⁹⁄₆₄)	⁵⁄₆₄	³⁄₆₄	¹⁄₃₂
#2	¼	³⁄₃₂	³⁄₆₄	¹⁄₃₂
#3	¼	⁷⁄₆₄	¹⁄₁₆	³⁄₆₄
#4	¼	⅛	¹⁄₁₆	³⁄₆₄
#5	¼	⅛	⁵⁄₆₄	¹⁄₁₆
#6	⁵⁄₁₆	⁹⁄₆₄	³⁄₃₂	⁵⁄₆₄
#7	⁵⁄₁₆	⁵⁄₃₂	³⁄₃₂	⁵⁄₆₄
#8	⅜	¹¹⁄₆₄	⅛	³⁄₃₂
#9	⅜	¹¹⁄₆₄	⅛	³⁄₃₂
#10	⅜	³⁄₁₆	⅛	⁷⁄₆₄
#11	½	³⁄₁₆	⁵⁄₃₂	⁹⁄₆₄
#12	½	⁷⁄₃₂	⁹⁄₆₄	⅛

NAILS

Nail lengths are identified by numbers from 4 to 60 followed by the letter "d," which stands for "penny." For general framing and repair work, use common or box nails. Common nails are best suited to framing work where strength is important. Box nails are smaller in diameter than common nails, which makes them easier to drive and less likely to split wood. Use box nails for light work and thin materials. Most common and box nails have a cement or vinyl coating that improves their holding power.

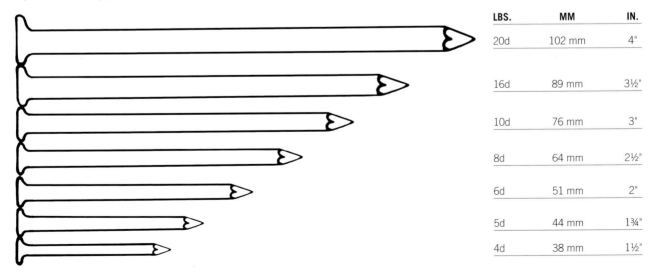

LBS.	MM	IN.
20d	102 mm	4"
16d	89 mm	3½"
10d	76 mm	3"
8d	64 mm	2½"
6d	51 mm	2"
5d	44 mm	1¾"
4d	38 mm	1½"

INDEX